How to Make Our Mental Pictures Come True;

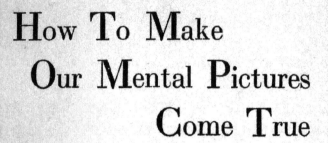

How To Make
Our Mental Pictures
Come True

A SERIES OF EASY LESSONS
IN THE ART OF VISUALIZING

BY

GEORGE SCHUBEL

L. N. FOWLER & CO.
7 Imperial Arcade, Ludgate Circus
London, E.C., England

———

PUBLISHED BY
THE ELIZABETH TOWNE CO., INC.
HOLYOKE, MASS.
1922

PREFACE

Among the imaginative stories of our childhood days, who does not recall the charm which Aladdin and his wonderful lamp held for us? How marvelous were the things which came to pass each time that he rubbed it! How often in our childish imagination did we wish for just such a wonder-lamp which would provide us with all the things which our hearts desired!

Yet this fancy of childhood is father to a wonderful scientific fact possible of being demonstrated mentally, and of being universally used to satisfy every requirement of the human heart.

We are each one of us a mental wonder-lamp manifesting a form of power more marvelous than ever was the light which shone from Aladdin's lamp.

What is this form of power of which we speak? For want of something more comprehensive we call it the visualizing power of the mind. Yet it is more than this. Its action involves a whole series of manifestations. We observe that it formulates, differentiates, specializes, chemicalizes and projects itself in us and through us, so that by means of it our hearts' desires are formed into thought-images, and then by a further process of differentiation and specialization they are projected and materialized until they become the visible objects of our *outwardly visible world.*

What do we know about the nature of this form of mental power? Very little. It is barely as yet within the grasp of our comprehension. But we have taken cognizance of its operation and results just as we have of electricity, radio-activity and other forms of power.

In what manner does it operate? The question is best answered by observing its inner-conscious, interconscious and objectively unconscious working in us and thru us.

In our lives we have noted very definitely that certain things which we have strongly desired and held as thought-images in our consciousness, have after a time " come true." From the seemingly invisible side of things they have made their appearance on the outwardly visible side of things. This is not a miracle. It is not some rare phenomenon.

It is not even unusual. It is simply the normal, continuous, unconscious functioning of this form of power.

Our natural desires are spontaneously and continuously shaping themselves into objects of thought, and these into thought-images which are being impressed, developed and reproduced outwardly all the time.

By its action upon mind-substance our desires, or mental images, become concrete, outward realities, visible to the physical eye. That is how *ALL THINGS* which we are able to see, touch and otherwise outwardly sense in this world have come into outward existence either in a universalized or individualized sense.

Heretofore, this formulative process has been largely a haphazard one. Our needs, for the most part subconscious, have simply brought this power into action automatically in a perfectly natural way, with more or less outward success. But now, in mental science, we have begun to study the process by watching its operation within ourselves and others, so that instead of an unregulated process it becomes one which can be regulated and controlled.

We have come to know the definite mental-mechanical action which is set in motion and the definite chemicalization which takes place; that these can be placed on a basis where they can be intelligently and deliberately controlled so that we are able first to *select* our desires; secondly to *consciously shape* these desires into objects of thought, and to establish them as thought-images in our consciousness; and then from this point on we can deliberately exercise this power so that what we desire and see inwardly, can be reproduced outwardly as a part of our outward world of things.

We are actually able to SEE *inner things into outward existence.*

There is no doubt whatever that this supreme form of mental power which we call visualizing, will be formulated finally into a definite and exact science to be used for all the legitimate purposes covered in this book, and in a consecrated way. May the following pages serve as definite outposts leading to this end.

—THE AUTHOR

INTRODUCTION

By Mrs. Genevieve Behrend

I FIND a definite joy in the fact that the first of George Schubel's series of books on visualizing has been put into printed form. There is a thirst for knowledge and an increasing need at the present day for books of this kind. Each day the study of mental science is becoming more and more resorted to by those persons who, discovering the futility of their struggle *against* the laws of our increasingly complex life of today, are learning to adjust themselves, and to work *with* these laws. When this is done they find that they are working in harmony with a power which enables them to accomplish what otherwise would be seemingly impossible things.

To those who are but slightly acquainted with the universal truths of applied mental science, I recommend this book. The author was one of my early students, and his own wonderful prosperity and success in business and financial affairs is, to my mind, the best demonstration of the facts which he offers to others in this present volume. He has given us a clear, analytical exposition of visualizing, and any imagined veil of mysticism which may have surrounded this subject in the past, has been removed under the strong and comprehensive light which he has thrown upon it.

In my own experience, visualizing for practical purposes came as an inspiration after reading Judge Troward's works on Mental Science. It provided the necessary means for my sojourn in England and my extensive studies as Troward's personal pupil, and, in the six years of my work in New York I have demonstrated the practicability of this power with most remarkable results personally and for others.

Visualizing is nothing more than the process of the impersonal, universal, unspecialized, undifferentiated Mind *seeing* itself into the specialized, the concrete, and the particular; bringing the inward seemingly unseen universe with all its multitudinous and ever-shaping forms into outwardly visible existence. It is a specialized operation from a specific center for the specific purpose of bringing substance into outward concrete form, and all that is necessary is for us to *personalize* this power for our particular needs.

When thus deliberately applied, visualizing can be made to do away with hospitals, asylums, prisons, charitable homes, and institutions now devoted to the correction of poverty, disease and crime. The desire of each individual heart whether for health, wealth, love, harmony, peace, beauty, happiness or whatever other form of good may be sought, can be materialized into the outward without breaking a single law of society, without injury to oneself or anyone else, or without taking anything away from anybody else.

Visualizing serves as the means of a never-ending source of supply for all. We are able to get all that we want out of the everywhere of substance from which our pictures take form. The limitlessness of what we may have out of this unlimited immensity is proportioned only by the limit of our own consent to or recognition of these resources.

In conclusion may I say that the time will come when visualizing will be taught in the schools and universities of the world as a natural science, thereby providing a single, direct and orderly means for securing all those

things of life which we need for our wel-
fare and happiness here. It is the greatest
effort and time saver that has so far come to
the consciousness of man because by means of
it, depending upon our ability of application,
we can *see* into materialization all those good
things which we now obtain by such laborious
mental and manual efforts.

CONTENTS

PART I. — MECHANICS OF VISUALIZING

PART II. — CHEMISTRY OF VISUALIZING

PART I

MECHANICS OF VISUALIZING

How to Make Our Mental Pictures Come True

CHAPTER I

PHOTOGRAPHY OF THE MIND

IN establishing a basis for the study of visualizing, we can think of no more simple beginning than to compare it to photography.

The theory, the mechanical principles and the technique applying to both are the same. Visualizing is the inner process, while photography merely is the outer process. Or we can say that the one is the hidden process, the other is the *hidden process revealed*.

In visualizing, a method of mental operation is employed which brings into play a group of principles operating innerly in mind; photography employs a method of operation which brings into play this same group of principles,

the difference being that they are operating
outwardly in reproducing outward things.

The various mental movements necessary in
reproducing the thought-images or mental objects of our consciousness are no different as
we shall see from the various movements
necessary on the part of the photographer in
reproducing an outer object.

Briefly stated, visualizing is an inner application of certain principles of which we can
become cognizant by observing the corresponding outer application which we call photography. In fact, photography is visualizing
made outwardly visible to our objective senses,
*it is visualizing visualized into outward form
so that outward things can be reproduced for
us in the same manner in which they are reproduced in the mind.* Hence, if we begin our
studies by an understanding of the theory and
working processes of photography, we will begin to understand the theory and working
processes involved in mental-photography, and
at the same time we will lay the basis for an
exact and definite science of visualizing which
will serve us at all times and for every purpose.

We know that when we apply the principles
of photography; when we operate the mechanical parts of the camera — the lens, the range-

finder, the shutter, in a certain way; and when we apply the proper chemical elements in a proper manner, then we are able to reproduce an object with unerring accuracy. So with the mental-mechanical and chemical principles and faculties involved in reproducing our desires and thought-images. When we apply them correctly we will get outward results that are just as definite, just as truthful, just as accurate reproductions as those produced by the intelligent photographer.

Of course, diligent study and application are necessary. The photographer could not be successful in his reproductions if he were not completely familiar with the essentials and methods involved in reproducing objects, and in the same manner we must be completely familiar with the essentials and methods involved in visualizing if we are to expect the same positive results. The law of cause and effect applies here as elsewhere.

In addition, we need to *believe* in the outcome of our work. Somewhat later we will touch more fully upon this point. Let us simply say here that we do not disbelieve the fact of photography; we do not doubt that its employment will bring about certain definite results in the matter of reproduction. So, as

we go forward in our studies we will find that
there is as little occasion to disbelieve the fact
of visualizing, or to doubt that its employment
in our affairs will bring about just as definite
results. For the present it is sufficient to believe that everything into which our desire can
fashion itself *already exists* and *has always
existed* as a paradigm in the pattern-mind of
the Infinite, otherwise it could not be conceived
or formulated in our own mind as an object.
We can refer to photography itself, for
instance, to make this more clear. The camera
first of all had to be an object in some one's
mind before it took outward form. Some one
thought of it, or in other words *pictured it*
before it could be assembled in the form of a
camera which we can touch and see. So with
all the other devices which are a part of
photography.

If then, the camera and all the other essentials of photography can reproduce and outpicture the object toward which they are directed, how much more easily is it possible for
the inner photographic equipment of the mind
under like suitable conditions to reproduce and
outpicture the object of our hearts' desire
toward which it is directed by means of proper
thinking.

CHAPTER II

SUBSTANCE OUT OF WHICH OUR MENTAL
PICTURES ARE MADE

BEFORE entering upon a study of the mechanical principles and technique involved in photography we are confronted with
the same necessity which confronts the really
good photographer. He must make himself familiar with the facts with which his mechanics
and technique must deal, and so must we. We
must familiarize ourselves with those mental
factors with which our mind-mechanics and
technique deal.

Let us see how this holds good in photography in order to apply it to our own study. We
know that in photography the very first of
these factors is *the object which is to be reproduced.* If the photographer has studied
physical science *he is familiar with the fact*
that this so-called object or concrete thing is
reducible by formula into a state of lesser and
lesser density until it can be resolved back to its
original state. He knows that if the formula

could be pursued, his object would be reduced to a point where it would become again a part of the universal substance to which physical science has given the name of ether. This all-pervading substance is believed to be the basis of all material objects.

The study of visualizing must be based upon the same hypothesis except that it goes a step beyond that of physical science, and refers to *a substance infinitely rarer as the basis of all things whatsoever hidden or revealed.*

The photographer, in pursuing his physical science studies is informed that the most distinguishing quality of this ether-substance is *light.* Wherever ether is, light is, and since this radiant ether-substance is everywhere present, light is also everywhere present in all the reaches and immensity of infinite space. In fact, physical science will some day accept the fact that there can be no substance without light, and no light without substance. It is only a difference of vibration and tenuity which makes the seeming difference between what we know as pure light and matter, and the student will so understand this when substance or light are hereafter interchangeably used.

In visualizing we learn this same fact about the infinitely rare, all-pervading, invisible substance with which we are to deal mentally, namely that its most distinguishing quality is this same *light* but in a mode of vibration infinitely rarer and finer than physical science can conceive. In fact, we are coming to find that what our very mind-substance is charged with is ambient quality in its purest state, acting upon, in, and through it. We speak of this "light of the mind" as being "above the light of the sun" in rarity; we speak of it as the "unseen light that never shone on land or sea;" and its wonderfully luminous power is implied when we say that a certain person has "enlightened" us, or when we say "light has been given us" or "light has been thrown upon the subject." Also, we speak of the "light of understanding," "the light of wisdom," the "light of faith," and of a number of other illumined mental conditions and activities qualified by this mental-light. The qualification in every instance is more than figurative. *It is scientifically correct.* So much so that we can say that this light of *wisdom, understanding and faith,* is not only a qualification but that it is mind itself, and the primary basis of all mind-substance.

So we can say that in the same manner in which the outward light serves as the luminous and vitalizing basis of the ether-substance from which all things of the visible universe, including our physical selves, are formed, so in an *infinitely rarer sense* does the invisible light serve as the basis of that radiant mind-substance which we call life, spirit, energy or consciousness, and out of this light, as we shall subsequently see, our mental pictures take form.

CHAPTER III

HOW OUR MENTAL PICTURES FIRST
TAKE FORM

THE photographer studying physical science finds that this universal light is not only the primary basis of universal substance but the forming, specializing, differentiating and projecting power as well. He finds that this universal light forever is acting in, upon and through the universal undifferentiated substance which it itself is, so that it is forever in a state of spontaneous formulation, taking shape and character out of its ambient being according to the initial impulse given to its movement.

In the most elemental physical sense then, we find an all-pervading infinite ocean of pure primary light, of an inconceivable rarity, continuously acting upon and within itself in the nature of a movement which we know as vibration, and which physical science first observes in the pure waves of light which are termed ether, and from this point it is more readily comprehended in its forever separative and outwardly appearing process, until the point where the photographer finds a universe and a world of outwardly visible objects toward which he can level his photographic camera for purposes of reproduction.

This is the manner in which *light takes on form* in the physical sense in which we recognize all outwardly visible objects including the immense universe and our more specialized selves; forever changing from the universal to the particular, from the unformed to the formed, from the undifferentiated to the differentiated, and from the unspecialized to the specialized. All visible objects are primarily of the substance of light, assuming shape and density according to the momentum of the outpush or initial movement coming from the invisible sense-world to the visible sense-world so that trees, persons, hills, stars, landscapes and all else visible are but the differentiated effects of the one primary light impulsing upon its own impalpable substance, and formulating itself into literal *objects of light* but so compactly that these objects become separately visible to us in contrast to the more general light out of which they have been formed.

Now then, in laying the basis for our visualizing studies, we go beyond these remotest points of physical science and of the senses, and apply this same observation in regard to light to the formation of our own selves. We say that the forming, specializing, differentiating and objectifying power, energy or life, call it what we will, is this same light operating in an infinitely rarer invisible and inner manner; forever acting upon, in and through its own unformed, unspecialized, and undifferentiated *universal conscious substance* so that it formulates, particularizes, specializes, differentiates and objectifies itself into individualized forms which we recognize as our individual objective selves or minds, shaping itself out of the *universal* objective sense-consciousness and becoming the individual objective sense-consciousness; becoming in fact our very inner selves — *objects of light* — and in turn we can say that within ourselves this same continuous separative process of the light goes on, so that out of our inner illumined selves are formed our objects of thought — objects of light, which we qualify by the term " bright " thoughts and by other terms descriptive of the substance of light out of which they are formed.

We become conscious of the initial movement or outpush of the mind-light substance
shaping itself through us in its most primary
sense as motion, commotion, or as we are accustomed to call it — emotion. When the impulse is forcible enough to motivate and sustain
itself, a differentiation takes place in the form
of what we call desire. If our desire is sufficiently strong and vitalized, a further differentiation of the mind-light takes place spontaneously or, in visualizing, *deliberately,* in
the form of our objective thinking; establishing itself in the objective state of our consciousness as an " object of light," an " enlightened "
idea or thought-object which, as we shall observe later, we are able to see within us by reflection and which by further specialization
becomes reproduced outwardly as a thing.
The process which results in this latter phenomenon is explained by the fact that the substance of light within the mind forms itself
outwardly by acting upon the substance of
light outside of the mind, and this is the manner in which it is assumed that our thought-
objects reproduce themselves in outward
visible form in the things which we desire.
  This formulation of the light-substance of

mind in us and through us is going on continuously and spontaneously. It is a characteristic of our being; we cannot be without
desires, and *we cannot experience a .desire
which does not seek to formulate itself into
some sort of objective thinking.* Our objective
thinking formulates itself into an objective
thought, and *we cannot know an objective
thought which does not move.to differentiate
tself from the inner invisible into the form
of the outward visible thing toward which our
desire primarily is directed.*

Our thought takes outward shape always
and for this reason it is scientifically correct
to say that " thoughts are things," fashioned
out of the only true substance of light out of
which all things whatsoever visible or invis-
ble are formed.

In *deliberative visualization* for certain
things of our hearts' desire, we do not seek to
change the natural spontaneous movement of
this invisible universal formulating, differentiating and specializing characteristic of the
light, life or energy acting upon and in and
through us, but rather to fulfill it.

To its activity we bring directivity; to its
spontaneity we bring regulation and control,

and in this manner we bring to ourselves all already existing things which relate themselves to our inmost desires, together with their circumstances and conditions, in an orderly and logical manner and in natural sequence.

CHAPTER IV

MIND'S PHOTOGRAPHIC STUDIO

IT is quite natural to understand that it would be of little value for the photographer to see and comprehend his object if he had not some sort of mechanical equipment with which to project, focus and reproduce what he sees. So, too, it would be of little avail for us to be able to formulate our mental objects, and to comprehend them if we did not have some sort of mental-mechanism by means of which we could reproduce outwardly the thought-images held within the mind.

For photographic purposes the photographer has a well-equipped studio provided with settings, camera and all other essentials and materials. A similar inner equipment of the mind is found in what we call our *objective state of consciousness* serving us as an elaborate mental photographic studio provided with all the mental-mechanical essentials and materials needed to image forth and reproduce our desires — our objects of thought.

31

CHAPTER V

TRUE CAMERA OF THE MIND

THE very first observation in comparing our mental-mechanical photographic outfit with the outfit of the photographer is that the group of faculties assembled and brought into play objectively in visualizing constitutes a mental device corresponding perfectly with the photographer's camera. It is in fact an *altogether true camera* with a mental-mechanism which operates *unerringly* in capturing thought-images whether ours or those of others; registering them faithfully upon the mind's sensitized film, and reproducing them true to their original form.

We find embodied in it all those subordinate and co-ordinate mechanical mind-principles such as the principle of the camera-eye, lens, dark chamber, tripod, enlarging device, range-finder, camera-shutter, film and the other contrivances which we know as a part of the camera.

In the manner in which the camera catches

up and specializes within itself the universal light of the sun, and forms it into the imprisoned light-images which upon development we know as photographs, so do the mechanical faculties which serve as our mental camera, collect together and specialize within our being the mind-light; shaping it into the thought-images which we recognize mentally.

The principles involved in the use of the inner camera of the mind are the same as in the outer photographic camera, serving to focus, concentrate, transmit, illumine, reflect and impress the object to be reproduced.

CHAPTER VI

MENTAL CAMERA-EYE

EXAMINING the photographer's camera in more detail, we find that its principal device is a lens or camera-eye situated in the very front of the camera.

This photographic lens is nothing more, we may say, than an outward embodiment or extension, in principle, of the more delicately fashioned lens of the physical eye, and the physical eye in turn is nothing more than the outward embodiment or extension in principle of the yet more indefinable single invisible " inner eye " or seeing faculty of the mind.

Just as the function of the lens of the camera is *not to see* but to serve as an instrument through which to see, so with the " single inner eye " of the mind.

In photography this is made possible in the following manner:

The fine rays of the sun are continually pouring themselves in a steady stream of light against the more solid substances of light which we call material objects. But these rays, in pouring themselves against these objects, are " thrown back " or deflected again into space. Now when the camera-eye is leveled in the direction of a given object, the light which is falling back from the object pours into the camera through the camera-eye. The lens of the camera-eye *collects, focuses* and *transmits* this light into the dark chamber where it is established in a manner enabling the photographer to behold it as *an exact light-image* or reflection of the outer object.

This is equally true of the physical eye. It does not *see* but simply serves the purpose of concentrating and transmitting the light-rays of the sun deflected from the object toward which our eye was directed, so that we can behold the light in its combined, collected, established and projected form in our minds, as the exact light image or reflection of the outer object.

Finally we find that the invisible inner " single eye " serves in a similar manner in the mental-mechanical arrangement used consciously or unconsciously in visualizing. The infinitely finer rays of our illumined objective thinking are continually pouring themselves in a steady stream of mental-light against the more solid mind-substance or " object of our thought." But as this stream of mental-light pours itself against the thought-object, it is thrown back or deflected, as it were. It is here that the invisible inner single eye of the mind catches, focuses and transmits this mental-light into the dark chamber of our being where it is assembled, so that the seeing principle within us is able to behold it as an exact light-image of the thought-object from which it is deflected.

Often the " light thrown upon a subject " existing in one mind is so illuminative that its reflection occurs not only in the mind in which the object of thought is being sustained, but in many other minds, so that the mental-light traveling from a person who is elucidating a certain thing will compel the exclamation " I see " from the other minds who have leveled and focused their inner mental eyes in the direction of the speaker's mind, and have thus caught the image in their own. The inner camera-eye of their minds has been able to *see* the objectified thought in its " true light " by reflection; it has been able to concentrate and transmit this light and reassemble it into a definite symbol or light-image capable of being recognized by them.

Like the eye of the camera, the eye of the mind in visualizing is or can be made perfect and true. It will collect, transmit, assemble and reflect for us whatever projected thought-object we deliberately may choose in our visualizing work for reproduction.

CHAPTER VII

DARK CHAMBER OF THE MIND

ANOTHER mechanical arrangement of the photographer's camera which serves to illustrate our study is found in the box-like compartment back of the camera-eye known as the " dark chamber."

We find a similar arrangement back of the physical eye by means of which we are able to observe, recognize and know the things of the outer world.

In turn the compartment in back of the physical eye is simply the outwardly fashioned " dark chamber " representing an inner state of consciousness which we are able to establish at will in the exercise of our visualizing power, and which serves as a mental compartment, so to speak, back of the single inner eye of the mind, so that we can say there is a " dark chamber " of our consciousness just as there is a dark chamber of the camera.

But in the same manner that the photographer has found it necessary to have an out-

38

ward arrangement of this principle in the form of a dark compartment in his camera, so in visualizing, at least in the beginning, we shall find it necessary to have some outward compartment representing this same inner principle; some quiet room in some part of the house which can be made as dark as possible, and which outwardly will be a counterpart of, and help to induce that darkened state of consciousness which is necessary in conditioning our mind for visualizing purposes.

Let us familiarize ourselves for a moment with the purpose of the dark chamber of the camera in order that we may understand the principle which it outwardly embodies.

The dark chamber shows the photographer the reflected light-rays which the lens of the camera has caught, collected and thrown into it as an imaged object of light. When he glances into it he observes this light-image by reflection; he obtains his perspective, his focus, by means of it, also he sees whether the proper quantity and quality of light is being reflected.

So with the state of consciousness of which the dark chamber of the camera is a counterpart. It shows us the reflected light-rays of our objective thinking which the inner single eye of the mind has caught, collected and thrown into our objective consciousness as an object of thought. In this state of mind we are able to see *by reflection* the object of our desires; we get our mental perspective, our focus, by means of this mental image; also it serves to tell us whether the proper quantity and quality of reflective thinking is present.

The " dark chamber " of a camera might with good reason be called the " illumining chamber " since it conditions the imaged object and shows it to the photographer as an object of light, wonderful to behold. Similarly when we enter our quiet darkened room and, by means of this room, into a place within our consciousness where all is quiet and subdued, we find ourselves peering within ourselves into what we might with good reason call the " illumining chamber " of the mind.

It is in this state of objective consciousness in which *reflection* of the object of our thinking occurs; in which we meditate upon and contemplate our imaged thought; in which we are able to get our proper focus toward our thought; our proper perspective toward it, and in which we are able to consider it " in the right light."

Somewhat later in our actual work we will give more attention to the manner in which our thought-image is brought into this il-lumined mental chamber, how it is there acted upon, and how it is subsequently developed. Suffice it here to say that the photographer would get a haphazard picture if he did not use this illumining chamber; if he did not peer carefully through it at the reflected object which he is planning to photograph. For the most part it would be ill-proportioned. Proba-bly the light-image would be too dim or too sharp, or out of focus, and so it is in the matter of holding our thought-object in that place in our consciousness *where it is subject to reflec-tion;* to meditation; to where we can get the proper " light upon it." If we do not see our thought-object by this means, it will be re-produced haphazardly as is now mostly the case in the spontaneous and undeliberated out-ward fulfillment of our inner desires.

In the illumining chamber of our conscious-ness, we must review our projected thought; we must procure our proper perspective of it and we must judge there and then whether or not it is really worth while to bring forth into outward realization.

CHAPTER VIII

WILL SERVES AS MENTAL TRIPOD

WE know that the photographer's tripod serves the purpose of steadying the camera during the time in which the outward object is being focused, concentrated and transmitted, and during the time in which the light-image of the object is being reflected and impressed. Upon the steadiness of this support the distinctness of the resultant picture depends.

As a mental principle, our fixed will, among other things, serves this same steadying purpose of the tripod, by holding our cameric faculties steadily directed toward the object in mind; by holding the object steadily in view during the time of focus and concentration, and by holding the mental light-image of our object in place during the time of mental reflection and impression.

It is upon the steadiness of this supporting phase of the will that the distinctness and good results of the final outward picture is obtained.

However, it is generally and mistakenly thought that this holding function of the fixed will necessarily implies a tensive effort or strain of the mind, extending even to rigidity of the muscles of the body, but this should not be the case. The holding of our projected thought should not and in true visualizing *does not* require any such mental state. It calls for an easy meditative holding of our mental object in place, and should be one of the most delightful phases of our visualizing work.

CHAPTER IX

MIND'S RANGE-FINDER

THERE is a function of the imaging faculty which, in visualizing, serves very much the same purpose as the range-finding device attached to a camera. Upon our *conscious* use of it later on in our visualizing work, much of our success will depend.

We know that the range-finding device of the camera serves as a measuring principle whereby the photographer's object is brought nearer to him and enlarged, or is made smaller and more distant. So the range-finding faculty of the mind will serve as a measuring principle, enabling us to view our mental object at will, or with all the breadth of vision which the unlimited consciousness of mind allows, and which we will learn to cultivate as our work goes on.

CHAPTER X

ENLARGING CAMERA-DEVICE OF THE MIND

THERE is an enlarging device attached to the more improved cameras whereby an object is seemingly brought nearer and enlarged to whatever extent the photographer wants his reproduced picture emphasized, or by means of which he can " bring out " this or that feature important to his picture as a whole. He is able to take the smallest picture and enlarge upon it to a degree where it can become, if he so desires, the major part of his reproduced picture.

In visualizing we bring into play a similar inner faculty which serves the very important purpose of bringing nearer to us and enlarging whatever good and desirable thing in our lives we would like to see expanded and made larger by means of reproduction; helping us to " bring out " this or that already existing feature of our present outward environment, circumstance or condition so that we are able to take the smallest object which gives us happiness and magnify it to a degree where it becomes the largest part of our reproduced mental picture.

In fact the easiest and most successful method of visualizing is contained in just this principle of enlargement. We take the most desirable things which are already a part of our outward lives, be they ever so small, and begin to see them in an " enlarged way." We find that it is easier to elaborate upon and idealize that which we already are, or possess, or have accomplished, than to formulate objects in our consciousness which may involve an entirely new set of circumstances and conditions.

CHAPTER XI

MIND'S CAMERA-SHUTTER

ANOTHER mechanical device which is a part of the camera, and which lends itself in illustrating the mental-mechanical apparata used in visualizing, is the shutter. This shutter, as we know, is immediately in back of the dark chamber of the camera, and separates it from the film.

Its particular purpose is to prevent the imprisoned light-image in the dark chamber from coming in contact with the sensitized film in back of it until released at the proper moment by the photographer.

Our will serves a similar purpose of protecting our unimpressed thought-image. Until we have properly examined our thought in the mind; until we have "looked into it" so to say; until we have gotten a proper focus and perspective of the thing which we want to be, or do or have; until we get the "right light" on it, the imaged thought is held from impressing itself upon the sensitive subjective film

47

of the mind by the will acting as the mental-
cameric shutter. Rapid as is the operation of
the mechanism of the camera's shutter, this
operation of the cameric faculty of the will
is instantaneous, except in those instances in
our deliberate visualizing where the time exposure is of advantage. Its manner of application will be touched upon later in our actual
work.

PART II
CHEMISTRY OF VISUALIZING

CHAPTER I

SENSITIZED MIND-FILM

W E have covered now fairly well the mechanics of visualizing represented by
that condition of mind which we know as the
objective *state of consciousness* but, like photography, *visualizing is essentially a chemical
process* which discloses itself best to us in that
phase of livingness of mind which we call the
subjective state of consciousness, and wherein
the wonderfully impressing, developing, fixing
and transferring of our mental images take
place.

Again using photography to illustrate this
chemical phase of visualizing, we find our very
first comparison in what is known technically
as the " sensitized " or chemicalized film. If
we were to examine this photographic film we
would find several very important facts about
it which will serve as the premise for certain similar facts relating to our subjective
thinking.

Our first observation is that the support of

the film is covered with a smooth plastic coating of gelatine in which has been mixed potassium bromide or sodium chloride, silver nitrate, and the addition of such other chemicals as may serve the purpose of increasing the sensitiveness and absorbing power of this jelly-like substance.

Our second observation, if directed through means of a high-powered microscope, would disclose to us the fact that the silver nitrate contained in this sensitized substance is made up of trillions of tiny electrons of silver evenly distributed and suspended in the interstices of the holding gelatine.

Our third observation deals with these silver electrons or units in themselves. On examination of them we would find that while they are in a whirling degree of velocity insofar as their own inherent movement is concerned, yet they are *static* or passive for the moment in their relation to external reactions. We say they possess *within themselves* all the principles of life in the sense in which we recognize and know life in outwardly visible movement, and potentially, in the sense of *action,* but as we said, they are for the moment in a quiescent or *subjectively active state.*

This is because the substance of the film in
which these electrons are suspended, is in itself
in a subjective condition, being carefully protected from the action of all outside light, and
this protection in turn serves in withholding
the electrons from either acting or being acted
upon.

Our fourth observation is that this jelly-like
substance of the film is *unformed* as yet. The
acting principle of formation is passive. It is
only at the moment when the photographer
allows the outside sunlight, in the form of his
imaged object, to impress itself upon the film,
that the formulating and specializing elements,
passive in the substance, and active in the light,
are introduced and begin their work.

Finally we can say of the plastic film-substance that it contains certain other qualities
such as permeability, impressibility, plasticity,
sensitiveness, retentiveness, as well as a " setting," absorbing, preserving and restraining
power.

In a very general way we can sum up by
saying that *the sensitized film of the camera
serves the purpose of receiving upon, preserving and subsequently developing* in its highly
sensitive substance the imprisoned light-image

which is drawn to it the moment the photographer presses the bulb, and releases it for the purpose of impression.

In conditioning our mind for the purpose of visualizing, we observe a mental-chemical or subjective element present which can well be compared to the sensitized substance of the film. The same peculiarly *permeable, impressible, plastic, sensitive* and *retentive* qualities are apparent which exist in the photographic film-substance, as well as the " *setting,*" *absorbing, preserving* and *restraining* power, so that we can well believe that the compounded photographic substance is only the more evident element of a like compounded mentochemical substance which exists in the subjective phase of our thinking. The student is asked to study and remember this phase of subjective thinking because of the peculiar properties which come into evidence and use in our later visualizing work.

If there were such a thing as an examination of the composition of this aspect of our subjective thinking, we would find among other phenomena that the trillions of tiny electrons of silver on the photographer's film have their prototype in what we may aptly term mentoids,

evenly distributed and suspended in the interstices of the plastic holding mind, if such a
distribution and suspension of mind-units is
possible to conceive. We would find further,
that while these mental units are in an incon-
ceivably whirling degree of life insofar as
their own inherent movement is concerned, yet
they are *passive* and *static* as yet in their relation to objective reaction, because protected
from and untouched by the objective thinking-
light, so that we can say the subjective state of
mind-substance of which these inconceivable
units are a part, for a moment neither acts nor
is acted upon.

Like the substance of the film, it is an *entirely passive substance.* Its unknown units
possess within themselves all the principles of
livingness in the sense in which we recognize
and know life in outwardly visible *movement,*
and potentially in the sense of *action,* but until
this subjective mode of thinking-substance is
brought in contact with, and acted upon by the
imaged object of mental light, it is in a merely
immotile and *subjectively* active state.

But the instant an objective thought is
transferred into the subjective state of our
thinking-substance, a formulating and special-

izing element,— passive in the subjective thinking and active in the thought itself,— is introduced which charges and changes the character of mind-substance, causing certain mental-chemical alterations to take place which will be touched upon later.

Finally, in a general way, we can say of the subjective state of mind, as we have said of the photographic film, that it serves the purpose of *receiving upon, preserving and subsequently developing* in its highly sensitive state the illumined thought-image which is released by the will from the dark chamber of objective consciousness for the purpose of impression.

CHAPTER II

MIND'S OBJECT OF LIGHT

PREVIOUSLY we have observed that all objects of a material or concrete kind, including the visible universe as a whole, if reduced to a primary state, would be found to be nothing else than a substance the basis of which would be pure light. From this light, all things are evolved, becoming specialized, differentiated, densified and objectified into the shape of the flower, the tree, the rock and all other outward forms whatsoever. We can say that all these outward things are merely embodied collections of sun-rays in different modes of vibration.

We have observed that the element of our thinking, if it could be reduced by chemical formula to a primary state, would be found to be nothing else than this same substance, the basis of which would be a light infinitely rarer and purer than the light with which we are familiar.

We have observed that this infinitely rare

thinking-light acts upon us, in us, and through us whether in a specific or universal way, for the purpose of formulation, making its movements apparent in what we call the emotions, then further generating itself in the elemental forms of desire, then densifying itself and taking form as mental objects of light in our sense consciousness providing they possess the structural and sustaining qualities which enable them to be built up in the shape of bodies or patterns of thought, just as we have learned that the external and cruder light of the sun takes form in the outer objects of which we are outwardly conscious. So we find that our rare, illumined thinking-substance becomes a self-lighted *object of thought* substantial in the degree in which our desire has vitalized it. We can say that all our thoughts are simply embodied collections of mind-rays in different modes or degrees of objective mental-vibration.

CHAPTER III

MIND'S IMAGE OF LIGHT

THE photographer in leveling his camera in the direction of any outward object is able to get a light-image in his dark chamber exactly like the object toward which his camera-eye is directed. We can say of this light-image as we said of the object itself, that it is merely an embodied collection of sun-rays but in a lesser degree of vibration and therefore not as substantial and solid for the moment as the object from which they are being reflected, but which later will be very tangible in the sense of a finished photograph.

By this we see that *the photographer does not photograph his object, but the sun-rays collected and assembled in his camera.*

When we level our cameric-faculties in the direction of our illumined mental object, we are able to get an image of mental-light in the illumining chamber of our consciousness exactly like the mental-object toward which our mental-photographic eye is directed. We can say of this mental image that it is simply an embodied collection of the mind-rays in a different mode of objective mental-vibration, and therefore not as substantial and solid for the moment as the mental object from which these mind-rays are being deflected, but which later will be very tangible in the sense of the outwardly finished and visible thing which originally was but a reflected thought in mind.

CHAPTER IV

MENTAL–CHEMICAL DEVELOPING AGENCIES

WE have said that the sensitized film in the camera serves, among other purposes, that of *developing* the photographic light-image impressed upon it. This we say is a process of " building up " the light image from matter *within* the film-substance; it is *an internal building up* out of the plastic substance itself, although it is a structural process of which we have no visible evidence when we look upon the impressed photographic film. It is not the entire developing process. So, in order to induce a complete outward photographic development, the photographer finds it necessary to supply matter external, for the moment, to the film-substance, and this is what may be termed a " building up " of the image from matter *outside of the substance of the photographic film*.

The photographer accomplishes this by what

MENTAL PICTURES COME TRUE 61

is known technically in photography as " developing agents " which will start into action a further chemical process of development, and in this wise " bring out " or make clear in detail the invisible light-image which is impressed on the film-substance.

However, these " developing agents " or substances are not used by themselves to produce development, but are mixed in certain scientific proportions so that a *compound* chemical developing substance is obtained, which mixed with water becomes the chemical bath or " developing solution " in which the photographer places his light-impressed film for further treatment.

We can say of the process that goes on in the developing solution, that it is simply a further formulative action of the developing principle inherent in the light-image, and which begins at the moment when the image is impressed upon the film, or we can say that it represents a further precipitation, or " building up " of deposit on the pure metallic silver electrons suspended in the sensitive film-substance, and serving as additional supply or *density* of silver metallic deposit to the " body " of the light image.

We can say that the solution is also a *liberating* and *freeing* agent, since certain of the chemical substances in it " liberate " the impressed image ; removing the bromide from the metallic silver deposit of the image, and " bringing it out " so to speak, in clear relief on the film.[1]

Like the sensitized film in the camera, so we have said of the sensitized and impressible state of our subjective thinking that it serves, among other purposes, the purpose of developing the illumined thought-image impressed upon this thinking, and we say of it that it is a mind-process whereby our mental-image is *" built-up " from a thinking within.* We underline and emphasize this point in order that the student may remember that there are two processes of development of our thought-image at work, one an inner mental process and one an outer mental process, as we shall see in a moment. These structural processes are really one and the same except that the beginning of the outward development of our im-

[1] There are, of course, various other chemical actions of a complex kind in connection with this developing process into which we cannot enter here without complicating our studies. We simply here touch upon enough facts to illustrate our lesson.

pressed thought is an *internal building up out of the plastic substance of mind itself of which we have no visible sense evidence for the moment.* So in order to induce a complete outward development into what we call matter, it is necessary to have matter of a kind external for the moment to the inner subjective thinking, and this is what we may term the " building up " of the imaged thought from material *outside* of our subjective thinking.

This is accomplished by mental " developing agents " which start into action a further mental-chemical process of development, and thus " bring out " or make visible in detail the invisible thought-image impressed in our thinking. These " developing agents " of mind in their compounded nature, constitute the mental-chemical bath, or developing solution of our sub-sense consciousness, in which our thought-image is placed. We can say with scientific correctness that in principle they are nothing different than the chemical developing agents which are used by the photographer.

Let us see if we can make this statement more clear by a simple study of one of the developing agents in the photographic solution such as the silver chloride or salts. In chem-

istry this substance can be reduced to finer
formulations which the chemist terms sub-
salts. Again these can be reduced to free lib-
erated vapors and gases. Beyond these he
comes to a non-formulative point where he
stops, and yet, by continuing the process of de-
duction we can follow the reduction from free
gases to a light-substance of yet finer modes of
vibration until in mental science we observe,
and recognize its mentative presence in what
we here term our sub-sense consciousness.

We can say of the developing process which
goes on when the imaged thought is transferred
to and sunk in sub-sense consciousness, that
it is simply a further formulative action of the
developing principle inherent in the imaged
thought, and which begins at the moment when
the thought-image is impressed upon the film
of subjective thinking; or we can say that it
acts as a further precipitation in consciousness; a further " building up " of the thought,
and serves as additional supply or *density* or
body to the thought in a manner which we shall
more fully cover in our later lessons.

We can say also that our sub-sense consciousness is a liberating and releasing agent, which
" brings out " our imaged thought, so to say,

in clear relief to a point where we can cognize
it by means of our senses.

Returning to the photo-developing solution
of the photographer, we observe that it is subject to and capable of various modifications
which are determined by the *quantity* or proportions of the developing chemicals used, or
by the presence of additional chemical agents.
These modifications are also induced by the
quality of the developing agents, or by what
chemists term the purity or impurity of the
ingredients. On these modifications depends
the clearness or unclearness of the final
picture; its detail or lack of detail, harshness
or softness, strength or lack of strength, tone
or lack of tone, density or faintness, vigor or
lack of vigor, perfection or imperfection, as
well as slowness or rapidity of development.

This is also true of the substance of our sub-
sense consciousness. It is subject to and capable of infinite modifications which are determined by the purity or impurity and the correct or incorrect proportions superimposed
by the kind of subjective thinking which we
are accustomed to do. On the presence or
absence of these modifications in our thinking
depends the clearness or unclearness of the

finished outer picture of the mind; its detail
or lack of detail, harshness or softness,
strength or lack of strength, tone or lack of
tone, density or faintness, vigor or lack of
vigor, perfection or lack of perfection, as well
as slowness or rapidity of development.

We cannot here go into details regarding
the various additional chemical developing
processes which the photographer finds necessary to completely develop his photograph, and
to give it permanence. It is necessary for him
to transfer his film from the developing solution to a clear water bath, then to a " fixing "
bath, then to a clear water bath again. After
this the film is thoroly dried and varnished.
The light-image on it is then transferred to a
sensitized paper similar in chemical composition to that of the film, and which is called
printing; then the print is immersed in a
developing solution and a fixing bath similar
to those in which the impressed film was previously placed. Here, too, various chemical
modifications are introduced in densifying and
modifying the impression.

Study of photographic development is dis-
closing constantly improvements which are
making this phase of photography truly an art

and a science of the highest kind. This fact is equally true of our visualizing studies. As stated in the beginning, these lessons are intended more or less to serve as outposts in this little known region of mental science, where only the wise men of the ages have penetrated. But there is no doubt that the study of mental-photography and particularly of the phase of it treated in this lesson, will make it an art and a science not only of the highest but also of the *most useful* kind in our human affairs.

Some day we will know how to get permanency, rapidity of action, lustre, tone, fixation, gradation, hardening, softening, retouching and intensification in our mental-photographic work as easily as the photographer is able to induce these various chemical modifications in his work. We have already seen that the photo-developing solution and fixing bath in which the photographer immerses his light-image, and out of which his photograph finally emerges as a real and tangible thing visible to the physical eye, is no different than the infinitely rarer compounded substance of subjective consciousness in which the seemingly impalpable thought-image is sunk, and out of which it materializes as a real and tangible thing visible on the outward plane of life. All that we must remember is that the various chemical processes, methods and improvements which the photographer uses in his developing work, and which are making photography an ever more and more exact science, *already exist as chemical principles in the laboratory of mind,* and that it is necessary only for us to *study and apply* these principles as they reveal themselves outwardly in the formulas which the photographer follows in order to get his same perfect developing results.

CHAPTER V

MENTAL–CHEMICAL PROCESS EXPLAINED

WE now have reviewed the chemical principles involved in visualizing, and now, in a general way, we will observe how these principles work out in connection with our visualizing studies.

Previously we have spoken of the light-image in the dark chamber of the camera, and of the thought-image in the illumining chamber of our consciousness. The manner in which both of these images are established is pertinent here.

When the photographer levels his camera in the direction of any outward object, the light-rays of the sun in falling back from the object are caught and focused by the photographic camera-eye, then transmitted to the illumining chamber, and there assembled, as we have observed, forming an *image of light* or *projected object* exactly like the object toward which the camera is directed.

This is precisely what takes place in con-

nection with the illumined mental-object in the
mind when our faculties become directed
toward it. If it has proved a pleasing or strong
mental excitant, if one can " sense " it strongly
enough, so to speak, it becomes held and established in consciousness, and we say that we are
" thinking about it."

The truth of the matter is that we are not
only " thinking about " it but *upon* it! It,
means that we are directing against our
thought, the vibrations or pulsations of a mind-
light much finer than our thought-object has
become, just as the unformed light of the sun
is a much finer light than the formed material
objects which were once a part of the sunlight.

The mental-light pours itself upon and
about our thought and bathes it just as the
cruder light of the sun continually pours itself
against all outward objects, and, in the same
manner in which the light-rays of the sun are
deflected from an object and thrown back into
space, so our objective thinking, in pouring
itself against the formulated mental-object in
the mind, is deflected and thrown back again
in consciousness.

However, here is where the wonder of the
mental-photographic process appears in strik-

ing contrast to the present photographic process employed by the photographer. If our object of thought is a strong enough excitant within us, a mind-heat is generated, the process of which we will explain later. The mind-heat gently and imperceptibly sets into movement the finely arranged and adjusted group of mechanical faculties which belong to what we call the " intellect," and which we have described as constituting the various parts of the camera of the mind; they become automatically and gently leveled in the direction toward which our attention has been excited, so that we are now focusing our mental-camera, so to say, in the direction of the mental object established in our sense-consciousness.

At the same time, in the manner in which the light-rays of the sun pour themselves upon the object and fall back, so our " thinking upon " and " about " our mental object is nothing different than the light-rays of our thinking which pour themselves upon our mental object, in the form of a continuous spray of mental-light, undifferentiated and unspecialized as yet in the sense of form. But when our mental-photographic eye becomes leveled against our object; when it catches and focuses this flood of deflected mental-light and transmits it into the illumining chamber of our consciousness, it becomes an *image of mental light* exactly like the mental object toward which our illumined thinking has been directed.

The light of our thinking takes shape; it becomes a *differentiated* and *specialized* form of mental-light, and by projection *it becomes in itself the mental object,* so that thereafter we no more deal with the object existing in our outer or sense-consciousness, but with the light which has formed itself as an image of the object, and which has established itself in the illumining chamber of our inner consciousness.

CHAPTER VI

HOW AN IMAGED THOUGHT IS
IMPRESSED

HAVING established his light-image in the illuming or " dark chamber " of his camera, the photographer presses the bulb, the cameric slide or shutter opens and closes according to the time of exposure required, and the wonder of the photographic impression is wrought.

The imaged light has streamed forward, and its actinic or chemical rays have penetrated and embedded themselves upon the highly sensitized and permeable substance of the film, and thus have become " impressed " in the exact form of the object which they imaged.

In a sense it may be said that a *form of sunlight is captured* by the photographer, and *is impressed into service* for his particular purpose of outward reproduction. It becomes temporarily an *imprisoned light* absorbed into the sensitive gelatine-substance of the film. In fact, the particularly concentrated chemical quality of sunlight out of which the light-image forms itself, becomes by absorption and penetration a part of the compounded substance itself, taking on its plastic body, and, by chemical affinity, affecting the marriage or union which results in the " quickening " of the light-image.

Simultaneously a transformation of the sensitive film-substance itself has taken place within the area in which the light-image has struck it. Its composition has become changed. The student will recall that previously it was an entirely *passive substance,* and that while the silver electrons distributed and suspended in it, possessed potentially all the evidence of life, yet this life was in a quiescent state. However, now by the vibrating energy of the light which passes into the substance with the entrance of the light-image, this substance has become converted from a passive to a magnetically active light-substance.

Also, we recall that the film-substance heretofore was an unformulated substance, but now the light-image has brought with it its own peculiar formulating and specializing characteristics so that at the moment of union the plastic light-substance develops a formulat-

ng and specializing power by means of which
the first stages in the development of the light-
image occurs within itself.

If this impressive moment could be observed
microscopically, we would find the electrons in
the streaming rays of light embracing the trillions of silver electrons suspended in the film-
substance, and in this union, effecting the
mysterious and subtile transfiguration which
chemists are unable as yet fully to explain.
All that they know is that the positive chemical
rays of the outer light have entered into and
impregnated the static electrons of silver,
merging with them by a process of smelting,
changing them to a more metallic quality, and
charging them with their own energy and
powers, so that these electrons develop a high
degree of whirling activity or " aliveness."
Heretofore passive, then, they have become
literally " enlightened " or " lightened up "
by contact with the imaged light, so that in
union with it, these tiny electrons of silver, as a
whole, become basicly the magnetic and metallic matter which forms the light-image in
the substance of the film, and which also later
will form the " body " of the developed film.

Speaking of the light-image we can say that

what has transpired at this moment of photographic impression is that a certain specialized form of outer objective light has passed into and become identified with a passive and highly impressionable film-substance, *for the purpose of becoming a more substantially specialized form of light,* and, for the time being it has become so *in an inner subjective sense;* we can say also that it is a differentiated form of light which has gone into and become identified with the inner undifferentiated substance on the film, becoming subjectively conditioned for the moment *in order to reassert itself in a further and more substantial differentiation of light* later on. It is, we may say, *a going inwardly* of this formulated, specialized, and differentiated light into the film, and becoming the active and magnetic element of its compounded metallic substance, so that it may again appear as light later on but in the denser and more permanent form of the finished photograph.

We dwell upon this transition here because throughout the entire visualizing process, as throughout the process of photography, we observe this phenomenon of specialization, differentiation and particularization in order to produce an ultimate result.

By this entrance into the film-substance the light-image is, we may say, on its way toward the *first stage of its outward tangible materialization or reproduction* as a photograph; it becomes a *more* tangible and substantial imaged object than when it was merely an image of pure light, because it has clothed itself now in a metallic body formed out of the enfilming and plastic film-substance in which it embedded itself.

It becomes now not only a further specialized and differentiated form of the sunlight as the photographer saw it in the illumining chamber of his camera a moment before, but it also becomes a *protected form of light,* pulsating at a different degree of vibration and energy now from that of the sunlight of which it was at one time a part, and for this reason the photographer carefully protects and seals the light-image on the film from contact with the external light-vibrations of the outer light until the darkened developing room is reached.

So with the illumined thought-image which is held in the dark chamber of the consciousness until released by the will or camera-shutter of the mind. It pours its formulated light-self upon the highly impressionable and

conditioned substance of subjective thinking;
in this permeable thinking-substance it becomes embedded and " impressed," and a
greater wonder than that of the photographic
impression has been wrought!

In a mentally scientific way we may say with
perfect correctness that the imaged thought is
a form of chemical mental-light which has been
captured by the mental camera-eye, and impressed into service out of the mind, whether
our own or that of another, for the particular
purpose of outward reproduction as a thing in
our lives.

The imaged thought for the moment becomes
an imprisoned thought. In fact, by penetration, absorption and embedment in the very
substance of subjective thinking, the thought
becomes a part of the compounded mind-substance itself, taking on its plastic, passive
qualities, and, by mento-chemical affinity,
causing a marriage or union of two phases of
thinking which results in a " quickening " of
the light-image in the mind.

At the same moment an alteration of the
subjective mind-substance itself takes place.
Within the area of mind affected by the in-
clasped thought-image, the thinking becomes

changed from a purely passive to a magnetically active mode. The mental-chemical elements suspended in this state of thinking we
can say have become " magnetized."

If we were able to observe these mental-
chemical elements at the moment of impression, we would see the trillions of tiny mentoids in an inconceivable whirl or state of
activity. Heretofore passive, these hardly im-
aginable units of the subjective phase of mind
have become electrified and " enlightened "
by contact with, and absorption of, the imaged
mental-light, so that now in affinity with this
light of the mind, they become the quickened
and basicly active magnetic substance of our
imaged-thought.

The thought-image takes on a state of extreme " aliveness." We can say that what
has occurred at this moment of thought-impression is this: A certain specialized form of
mental-light, which we call an imaged thought
reflecting our outer or objective mode of thinking, has passed into and become a part of the
inner highly impressionable mode of thinking-
substance which we term the subjective mode
of mind, in order to become a *more substantially specialized form of thought,* and for the

time being, it has become so in an inner subjective manner; we can say that a differentiated
form of thought has gone into and become a
part of the inner undifferentiated phase of our
thinking-substance in order to come forth
again in a further, ever different outward and
more substantial form of the thought or thing;
a going inward into mind-substance in order to
reappear in the outward as subjective mind-
substance itself, but in the denser, compounded
form of matter which subjective mind-substance is caused to become in its outward
formulation and expansion when acted upon
by the objectively imaged thought.

Also we can say that by this mental process
of impression our imaged thought is on its way
toward the first stage of its outward tangible
materialization or reproduction as a *thing, a*
circumstance, or a condition of outward life.
It becomes a more tangible, palpitating, vitalized and magnetic object in the consciousness,
than when it was simply a reflected object of
mental light, because the thought has now tak-
en for its living body the enfilming and plastic
substance of the subjective state of thinking
in which it has embedded itself.

It becomes now, not only a specialized and

differentiated form of mind-light, but it also
becomes a *protected form of mental light,*
highly sensitive, highly susceptible, highly
magnetized, and we may say, further differentiated from the objective mind-light which
was seen in the illumining chamber of the
mind; pulsating at a different degree of
mental vibration from that of the general
outward mode of objective thinking. It must
be kept from contact with, or exposure to
the kind of mental-light which is represented
in the external vibrations of the outward
method of thinking, whether emanating from
our own or other minds. The imaged thought
which was at one time a part of *objective
thinking* now becomes a part of what we
know as *subjective thinking,* and so must not
come in contact with the former at this stage
of the visualizing process. For this reason the
impressed thought-image is carefully protected and sealed with the will as we shall
subsequently see.

It is now a mentally-photographed thought,
a living object of the mind, forming itself out
of the filmy and plastic texture of subjective
mind-substance. Thereafter it will take tangible shape in sub-sense-consciousness, awaiting

333

333

33333333333333

only time and the proper mental conditions for its fixation, hardening, transference and outward development into the visible sense-world, where we can feel and see and otherwise become cognizant of it.

We can say of the thought-image what the photographer is able to say of his light-image, that it is on its way toward the first stage of its outward tangible materialization or reproduction as a mental photograph, and when we understand this *consciously and fully,* then all doubt about the reality of the mental-photographic process will cease.

We have only to consider the fact that the photographer's film has impressed upon it nothing more than a collection of light-rays, nothing more than a light-image offset by a shadow, and which is altogether invisible to the sense-sight, yet when he subsequently applies the appropriate developing process to it, he finds that that which for the moment is invisible on the sensitive surface of the photographic film gradually formulates itself into that which is visible to the eye.

It is a marvelous fact yet perfectly natural in both instances, and that which is true of the photographic film is just as true of the subjective impressionable element of the mind of which the film is the outward chemicalized correspondent. Our heart's desire forms itself into that which is but a thought at first; the thought becomes projected and impressed upon our subjective thinking and by the process of development next to be explained, becomes the thing which is visible to our eyes.

CHAPTER VII

HOW AN IMPRESSED THOUGHT PASSES INTO MENTAL SOLUTION

THE photographer carries his photographic film, with its impressed form of sunlight, to the developing room, and here places it in the " developing solution." This for the purpose of further development. It is necessary for the light-image to continue along the lines of its peculiar formative power, since we must remember that, after impression, the image becomes not only a vitalized and magnetic image, but continues to be a *formulative* one, even though its forming power has become changed now from a positive to a subjective one. However, the light-image of necessity must have something to act or work upon in order for its formulative power to exert itself, and this is why the photographer places it in the chemical developing solution. When he does this, we say that certain chemical actions and reactions or sensations take place in both the electrons which compose the metallic substance of the

84

light-image now, and the floating electrons in the solution, resulting in changes in both.

The first change is that caused in the substance of the solution by the light-image. We said previously that this substance in solution, like the substance on the gelatine film, originally is an entirely *unformulated substance*. However, now, as a result of the placing of the light-image in it, the formulating and specializing element of the light is introduced, and again manifests itself as it did when the light became impressed previously upon the film-substance so that we can say the solution is in process of becoming a formulated substance due to the presence of the imaged light in it.

This formulation does not occur, as in the instance of the film-substance, by the *positive* action of the rays of light rushing to, and penetrating the silver electrons in the solution. We must remember that this light is *subjective* now, having partaken of the nature of the film-substance in which it is embedded, so that now its formulating power acts as a purely *magnetic* or *drawing force* in connection with the formulation going on in the solution.

We remember the solution to have been an entirely *passive substance;* that its activity was

latent, and that while its free floating electrons
of silver possessed potentially within themselves the elements of livingness, yet, like the
electrons in the substance of the film, they were
in a *subjective* or *static state* of being. However, now, by a chemical reaction or sensation
very complex and difficult to trace, probably
by a transmission of the vibratory energy of
the light, these electrons become " polarized "
or *positive* in their nature, when the light-
image is introduced, and so the substance of
the solution becomes an *active substance objective in its direction.*

But this now active or positive substance
which the solution represents, must also of
necessity have something to react or work
upon, even as the light-image, and what is
more, it must have something which will draw
it forth, or attract it; something to which it
can respond or to which it can *give itself* since
that is now the nature of this substance.
Hence the reaction to the light-image which
the photographer introduces.

If during this further developing process,
the photographer again peered through a high-
powered microscope, he would see this chemical
action and reaction in the form of the trillions

of tiny " magnetized," metallic electrons of the light-image, whirling at an inconceivable degree of velocity in the substance of the film, and pulling toward them the trillions of " polarized " or positively active electrons of silver in the developing solution.

At the same time he would see the " polarized " or positively active electrons pulsating and stirring into movement; yielding themselves and rushing forward with equal velocity in response to the pull of the film-electrons, as if eagerly taking their appointed places in the substance of the light-image, or areas of light-impression into which they are reciprocally and rhythmically drawn.

We will remember here that the *depth* or *density* of the light-image formed originally in the substance of the film at the moment of impression depended upon the penetration of the image into the film-substance, and this penetration in turn depended upon the quality and quantity, or rather *intensity* of the light which was projected. Now, however, the additional depth or density of metallic deposit on the light-image will depend upon the quality and quantity of the substance of the solution, plus the quantity and quality, or intensity of the light which was projected.

In other words, if the impression of the light upon the film has been sufficiently intense, then there will be both depth and density in the form of the silver electrons on the film which has been penetrated, and if the solution is sufficiently strong, then this depth and density of formulation will be augmented by the further metallic deposit of the positive silver electrons in the solution.

We can say that this phase of the photographic developing process is a further densification of the light-image; a more concrete form of specialization; it is in fact *a further going-in process of the differentiated light-image* so that it may come forth again into the outward in yet more permanent and substantial form than before.

The final chemical change which we note at this time in connection with the photographic developing process is the " liberation " so-called of the projected light-image. As we have said, it has been captured, impressed, imprisoned and hidden in the compound film-substance. But now, due to the liberating agent present in the solution, all the temporarily withholding or restraining elements in the substance, as well as those unrelated and unessential to the specific image, become gradually removed from within and around it, " releasing " the impounded image and " bringing it out " from the surrounding film-substance.

Following this come the various chemical modifications and additional treatments of the light-image which the photographer introduces in the course of the developing process for the purpose of " hardening " and bringing forth into the visible a perfect and permanent print or reproduction of his object.

We are able to see, moment by moment, this chemical transformation take place, in the nature of a body of light, entirely invisible at first, gradually shaping itself in denser and denser formation of metallic substance, until, wonder of wonders, we behold becoming evident on the chemicalized paper, the finished photograph of a landscape, a face, a home, or whatever else was intended to be outwardly reproduced.

We now study our photographed *mental object* or *thought-impression* under a similar process of developing and at the time when it passes into the solution of our sub-sense consciousness.

It is necessary for our impressed thought-image to undergo a further process of development and to continue along the lines of its own peculiar formative power, inherent in itself, since, after the impression, the mental-image becomes not only a *vitalized* and *magnetic* thought, but continues to be a *formulative one,* even though its forming power has become changed now from an objective to a subjective one.

However, our impressed thought must have something to act or work upon in order for its formative power to exert itself, and this is why it becomes transferred and sunk in the mental-chemical developing solution of sub-sense consciousness. When this takes place we can say that certain mental actions and reactions or sensations take place both in the nature of our impressed thought and in the sub-conscious thinking in which it is placed.

The first mental change which we will note here is that caused by the action of the thought upon the substance of our subconscious thinking. We said previously that this thinking-substance, like the substance of the outer or objective phase of thinking, originally is an entirely *unformulated mind-substance.* However, now, as a result of the entrance of the imaged or projected thought into it, the *formulating* and specializing characteristic of the thought itself is introduced, and again asserts itself as it did when projected and impressed previously upon our subjective-thinking, so that we can readily say that the sub-sense consciousness is now in a process of formulation due to the provocation of the imaged thought present in it.

This subconscious mind-formation does not occur, as in the first instance, by the *positive* action of the mental light of our objective thought penetrating and permeating the subconscious mind, since our imaged thought is *subjective* now, having partaken of the nature of the subjective mode of thinking in which it is embedded, so that now the formulating character of its light acts as a purely *magnetic* or *drawing* power in relation to its own development in subconsciousness.

But the reverse of this becomes true of subconsciousness itself. We recall the fact that this state of our thinking is primarily a passive or static state of mind-substance; that its activity while eternally present is latent, and that while the free floating monads of subconsciousness possess within their natures all the elements of livingness, yet, like these same monads in subjective thinking, they are primarily in a *subjective* or *static state* of being. However, by a mento-chemical sensation or reaction which the mental scientist can but vaguely trace in his deductions, but which he can assume with reason is caused by a transmission of the energy of the objective mental-light introduced with the submerged thought, these mental monads become " polarized " or *positive* in their nature, and so we can say that the plastic subconsciousness affected by our thought becomes an *active formulating and specializing* mind-substance, *objective* in its direction. It becomes quickened into an area of extreme activity, proportionate to the strength and vitality existing in and introduced by the impressed thought.

But this now active or positive area of subconsciousness must of necessity have some sort of thinking-substance on which to react or work, and what is more, it must have some kind of thought which will draw it forth or attract it ; some thought to which it can respond or *give itself,* since its *givingness* has now become active, and this implies action. Hence its response to the projected thought which has been introduced into it.

If during this continuity of development of our impressed thought, we were able to see the mental-chemical actions and reactions going on, we would observe the uncountable trillions of " magnetized " mentoids composing the imaged thought, whirling with inconceivable *subjective* velocity, and drawing toward them the uncountable trillions of " polarized " or *positive* mentoids in subconsciousness.

At the same time we would see the " polarized " mentoids pulsating into movement; *yielding themselves,* and rushing forward with more ethereal rapidity and ease than the electrons in the photo-solution; giving themselves in response to the *pull* of the subjective mentoids, and eagerly taking their appointed places in the area of the thought-impressed substance into which they are reciprocally and rhythmically drawn.

What is more, this activity is not confined to the limitations of a certain area allowed by a photographic film, or a certain quantity of chemical solution or substance, as is the photographic process of a photographer, nor is it confined even within the limited scope of our

own individualized objectively and subjectively conditioned mind. Our illumined
thought passes on and beyond the limited scope
of our own circumscribed subjective thinking,
and becomes an enfilmed form of mental light
sunk in the great universal everywhere of subjective consciousness, formulating its structure of infinitely delicate thought-texture out
of the body-forming substance which underlies
and invisibly pervades all conditions, all circumstances and all affairs of the outward
world, including ourselves, so that friends,
relatives, strangers, words, occasions, circumstances, conditions and all else having mental
kinship, and coming within the magnetic area
of our impressed thought, will be attracted to
us in a seemingly miraculous, yet perfectly
natural way, in order to help us fulfill, and in
some instances to become a part of, our outwardly forming picture.

We will find thoughts similarly conditioned,
infusing and blending with our own, just as
the electrons in the photographic pan move
toward, infuse and blend themselves with the
magnetic electrons on the photographic film —
governed in both instances by the unerring law
of attraction which brings together all that

which belongs together — so that in the case of our developing picture, all that which belongs to it will eagerly, or should eagerly, find its appointed place as a part of it.

In a word, our immersed thought arouses and draws unto it a whole system of subconscious activities, and it is in this way and no other, that the chemical structure of our lives, of our mental images, shape themselves *out of the seemingly invisible everywhere* and finally reveal themselves to us *in the visible here* in the shape of the business, the home, or the simplest object which in thought we have sufficiently impressed upon the mind and chemicalized into outward form.

Let us note here that the *depth* or *density* of our thought-impression depends upon the degree to which it penetrated our subjective thinking, and this penetration in turn depends upon the *quality and quantity* or rather the *intensity* of the thought which was projected. We will touch upon this point in more detail in our subsequent lessons.

The point to be brought out here is that the *additional* depth or density of deposit on the thought, now depends upon the *quality* and *quantity* of the substance of our subconsciousness, plus the intensity of the impressed thought.

In other words, if the impression of the projected thought upon our subjective thinking has been sufficiently intense, then there will be both depth and density in the form of the mentoids which have been penetrated, and if the subconscious mind-solution is sufficiently strong, then this depth and density of formulation will be augmented by the further deposit of the positive mentoids of subconscious mind.

We can say here that this phase of the mental-developing process is a further densification of our developing thought; a more concrete form of mental-specialization; it is in fact *a further going-in process of the projected thought* for the purpose of further mind-differentiation, so that it may come forth again into the outward in yet more permanent and substantial form than before.

The final mental-chemical change which we here observe in connection with the mental developing process is the " liberation," chemically speaking, of the projected light-image. As previously observed, our projected thought has been " captured " out of the infinite everywhere of objective thinking or more directly

out of the objective thinking passing through
us or another; it has been impressed, imprisoned and hidden in the enfilming substance
of subjective thinking. But now, due to the
liberating presence or intelligence made active
in subconsciousness, all the temporarily withholding or restraining elements of mind, as
well as those unrelated and unessential to the
specific thought, become gradually removed
from within and around it, " releasing " the
impounded thought, and " bringing it out "
from the surrounding compounded thinking.

Following this come the various mento-
chemical modifications and additional treatments of the thought which are consciously or
unconsciously introduced in the course of its
developing process, and which serve the purpose of " hardening," and bringing forth into
the outwardly visible, a perfect and permanent
reproduction of the thought or object originally held in the mind.

We shall see in later lessons how it is made
possible for the transformation of a thought,
in the form of a mental-body of light, entirely
invisible in the beginning, gradually to shape
itself in denser and denser formation of mind-
substance to the point of what we call matter,

until, greater wonder than the wonder of the photographic solution, we behold becoming visible in our lives, the outward evidence of our inner thought, of our mental picture, embodied in the substantial form of money, home, business, position, lover, husband, wife, friends, circumstances, conditions, or whatever else was intended by our desire to be outwardly reproduced.

CHAPTER VIII

DEVELOPING ROOM OF THE MIND

WE have stated that the photographer takes his impression or " negative " for development to a carefully darkened room called the " developing room." It is simple in arrangement, containing usually a chair, a pan holding the photographic solution, and a small, dim, red light, as an aid in observing the development of the photographic impression.

The room is darkened for the same reason that causes the photographer carefully to protect and seal his impression until the dark room is reached. The impression, as we know, is now a specialized and preserved form of light-substance, highly magnetized, sensitive and impressionable. It must be kept from contact with, or exposure to, external light-vibrations.

For this reason the photographer carefully boards his windows and doors, excluding every possible ray of outside light which may filter in and spoil the photographic impression.

In visualizing, the quiet, darkened room in which we carry on our work now becomes our developing room. Here we enter inwardly into a condition of consciousness which is similar in principle to the developing room.

The room in which our thought-developing is accomplished must be darkened for the same reason which causes us unconsciously to carefully protect and seal with our will, the impression of our projected thought until development has taken place. It is now, as we know, a specialized and preserved form of thinking-substance, highly sensitive and impressionable, and highly magnetized. Like the photographic film, it must be kept from contact with, or exposure to, the external vibrations of objective thinking of our own or other minds.

The darker the room can be made the better it will serve its purpose of providing outwardly the condition which we mentally need. It must more than ever be a " silence room " as well as a darkened room, since at this time we are providing an outer environment which corresponds with and provides the tone and atmosphere for our subjective mental condition, and from which must be excluded not only light-reactions which peculiarly affect our mental state, but those of sound as well. In fact, no sense-distraction or disturbing external vibration of any kind must be permitted to enter.

If a " silence room " or retreat of this kind cannot be provided, then as in the instance of the dark chamber, we must arrange to make our bedroom the place for treating our thought. In the hushes of the night, in the very early hours immediately after midnight, our best mental developing work can be done, since the outer objective vibrations are at their lowest.

An ideal " silence room " in itself can be made a first object upon which to visualize if we are not provided with such, so that through visualizing, we may so shape the circumstances and conditions of our homes that a " silence room " for all visualizing purposes may be secured.

CHAPTER IX

SUBSCONSCIOUS DEVELOPING PROCESS
EXPLAINED

W E recall that the first stage of the development of a photograph occurs when the outer light-image is let into and strikes the film substance. Immediately there occurs a reduction and conversion of the silver electrons suspended in the substance so that they become an unseen metallic basis or body incorporating the light which has penetrated and become part of them. We said that this was development from *within* the film substance.

We compared this with our objective projected thought, or rather with the formed light of our objective understanding, saying that the first stage of its development begins when our imaged-thought impresses itself upon our subjective thinking-substance, and that we call this the *inner* development of our thought.

The *outward* and *further* process of photographic development occurs as we have seen, when the photographer places his photographic impression in the chemical solution. The objective and positive light-image which became *subjective* and *magnetic* when it became imbedded in the photographic film-substance, now draws its further metallic " deposit " from the photo-chemical solution.

The *subjective* electrons or " deposits " in the photographic solution, we explained, become *positive* with the introduction of the light-image, and respond to its drawing power. In this way, we said, the subjective light-image draws to and gathers about itself a chemical structure or deposit out of the objective or positive substance of the chemical solution which is now subjectively controlled.

This metallic deposit, drawn from the solution, comes more and more into visible evidence until the complete picture is outwardly disclosed.

Speaking now of our imaged thought or form of understanding, we said that its *outward* and further development occurs the moment it is transferred to the subconscious levels of our thinking. For purposes of emphasis, we recall the fact that our projected understanding or thought undergoes a peculiar transformation before it reaches this *outward* stage of development. Originally it is an imaged *objective thought* of a mental object, then passing into our subjective thinking it becomes an imaged and impressed *subjective thought* or form of understanding of which we become *objectively unconscious and subjectively conscious.*

It is this originally *objective* and *positive* form of understanding, which became *subjective* and *magnetic* the moment it became imbedded in subjective-thinking, that we now find drawing its further deposits from the mind solution which we call subsense-consciousness. These " deposits " of mind become *positive* with the introduction of the projected thought, and respond to its drawing power. In this way, we said, our enfilmed subjective thought-image or understanding draws and gathers together around itself a chemical structure or mental " deposit " out of the objective or positive subconscious substance which our thought subjectively controls. Infinitely rare and invisible at first, this " deposit " becomes more and more a visible process, manifesting as persons, things, circumstances and conditions, until the complete mental picture is outwardly reproduced.

It is difficult to get across to the student a thorough comprehensive idea of what is really meant when we speak of a subsense-consciousness, in which the imaged and impressed thought sinks itself for the purpose of further outward development. We can think of the subsense-consciousness as a mental-chemical developing solution, and in the sense of an underlying body-forming mind-substance of such infinite rarity that it is inconceivable for us to form any conception of it, and from this state we can think of it as being embodied in all the forms and expressions of outward objective life.

We are individualized, not individual *units, of this subsense-consciousness. We are individualized only in the sense that we are* expressions *or manifestations of it, but not separate from it, so that when we say our projected thought or understanding is transferred or placed into our subconsciousness, it means that it becomes sunk* not in an individual subconsciousness *but rather in a universal, unlimited ocean of subjective or static consciousness everywhere present, and in which we move and have our being. It is thus that our imaged or projected understanding passes into subconsciousness subjectively drawing or pulling to it all that it needs in the sense of material, or substance, or " body " for its outward development, and from a depth limited only by the reaching influence and magnetic drawing power possessed by our understanding.*

We said in a previous lesson that the *density of deposit* drawn out of the *photographic solution,* and which settles upon the metallic electrons on the film-substance, depended upon the *depth* of the impression made upon the plastic film-substance, and that *this depth depended upon the intensity* with which the imaged light strikes the film.

So also, we said that the density of mind-deposit drawn out of the subconscious by our understanding depends upon the depth of the impression made upon our subjective thinking, and that this depth of impression depends upon the intensity with which our understanding or projected thought penetrates this thinking-substance.

If the formed light of thought is sufficiently intense, strong, and sharp, implying a pure, full and sufficient understanding or projection of the mental object, then its impression will be deep, and, correspondingly, its drawing power, when transferred to the subsense-consciousness also will be far and deep-reaching.

Here in these deeper levels our subjective understanding recognizes and finds at its disposal all the unknown and forgotten contents and treasures of thought, all the teeming psychic activities of life, all the wisdom and experience of untold ages which has sunk to lower levels in the course of time. It is these which *contain* and which *are* all the material and substance of our subsequent outward picture. It is these which are in a subjective or static state of being in this ocean until " quickened " into objectivity by that mysterious transmutation of vibrating energy which our illumined thought brings with it, and it is these which are drawn to our understanding out of these deeper levels to the level of our objective consciousness where they become the dense " deposit " which settles upon and around our projected thought.

In photography certain chemical agencies are introduced into the compounded photographic solution which, combining with the other chemicals in the solution, produce modifications in the developing process, so that in

one instance the light-image will be caused to
" flash up " all over at once, " bringing out "
the details quickly, and, in another instance
a certain chemical agent will bring out the
high-lights of the image first, while the gra-
dations or modified parts, or details, do not
fully appear until the general outlines are
somewhat developed.

Similarly, in principle, there are mental-
chemical agents within the compounded solution of subsense-consciousness, some of such
infinitely fine and imperceptible elements of
mind that we can know of them only by the
mental-chemical actions and reactions going
on within our own and other minds. Others
we recognize in the underlying actions and reactions afforded by circumstances, conditions
and the more visible things of outward life.

Just as the photographer has access to the
chemical developing agents, and to the
knowledge of their application for producing
his modifications, so have we mental access
to the mental-mechanical principles, and to the
intelligence whereby these principles can be
applied for the purpose of modifying and
regulating the development of our mental
picture.

CHAPTER X

HOW OUR INVISIBLE THOUGHT
DEVELOPS OUTWARDLY

IN the photographic developing process, as we previously explained, there are present certain physical laws represented by time and temperature in developing, quantity and quality of the solution, and by the re-actions and actions of certain chemical com-binations either naturally within the com-pounded developing solution or introduced into it by the photographer. These laws re-solve themselves into *formulas for developing.*

If these formulas or conditions are intelli-gently provided for by the photographer, then his part of the work of further development is for the most part completed. Thereafter it is not he who is bringing about results. The law of development, inherent within the im-pressed light-image is at work. *It is working for him,* gathering together a chemical struc-ture around the enfilmed image of light. His attitude becomes one simply of *co-operation.*

HE

He may lift the submerged film occasionally
from its chemical bath and carefully review
its progress, or see if his formula has been
carried out correctly; he may strengthen or
modify the solution according to the needs of
the developing picture, but aside from this
he knows that his treatment of his photographic impression has incited into motion
the characteristics of the impressed light; he
has started the process of formulation, specialization, and differentiation which will operate
unerringly in bringing about a given result.

In the mental-photographic process of developing our reflected and impressed thought,
there are, of course, certain *mental laws* which
serve as *formulas for developing*. If these
formulas or mental conditions are intelligently
provided for by us, then our part of the
mental-developing work is for the most part
completed. Consciously and objectively it is
not we who are developing results at this point
of the developing process of our submerged
thought. The law of development inherent
within our understanding and within our
thinking-substance is working subjectively
for us, gathering together the " deposit "
or infinitely delicate chemical structure around

the enfilmed mental-light which our under-standing has become. Our attitude becomes one simply of co-operation.

Occasionally we may consciously take our submerged thought-image from its mental-chemical bath; we may carefully review its progress mentally or see if our visualizing formula has been carried out correctly; we may strengthen or modify the subjective con-dition according to the needs of our develop-ing thought-image, but aside from this we know that our treatment has started in motion a characteristic of our impressed un-derstanding, resulting in a process of formu-lation, specialization and differentiation which will unerringly bring about the given results.

Once our understanding-thought has been projected into our subconsciousness, it finds in this mental-chemical solution an infinitely rare, underlying body-substance by means of which it can formulate itself, and through which it can move and extend itself in the di-rection of its outward fulfillment, going be-yond the limits of our own individualized sub-jective condition of mind and out into the un-limited ocean of Universal Subjective Mind in which all of us are, and we can assist only by

moving in the direction in which our developing thought moves us.

When we realize that this principle of development is working for us in the manner in
which we have described, then all anxious
thought on our part will cease, as to " how "
or " when " our thought is to materialize or
the means to be employed.

The fact is we should never in visualizing
attempt to define the manner through which
our projected thought will make its outwardly
visible appearance.

The ten thousand dollars we seek to visualize may come as the result of the death of a
rich uncle; it may come from the sale of a
piece of property; it may come from a friend
seeking an investment through us, or it may
come to us through the most remote, inter-
mediate and unexpected source.

All that we know, and this with unerring
certainty, is that the condition, the avenue,
the means available and susceptible are open-
ing themselves to provide for the development
and appearance, on the visible plane, of our
invisibly developing thought.

CHAPTER XI

POSSIBLE TO REVIEW A DEVELOPING MENTAL PICTURE

IN observing the photographer sitting quietly in his developing room, we see that occasionally he lifts his picture carefully from the pan in which it is being bathed, examines it, dips it back again and again in the chemical solution and so watches the orderly progress of its outward development.

His action suggests to us the fact that we will have this same privilege of reviewing our outwardly developing picture. In our quiet retreat, our darkened " silence room," we will find occasion to meditate upon our picture, bringing it before us for review as a whole. While we speak of our " silence room " for this purpose, let us remember always that our true " silence room " and " developing room " into which we are to enter, is in that place in the everywhere of subconsciousness where our picture will be placed, and in every part of that everywhere to which our picture may ex-

tend. If our minds are thoroughly trained in
the habit of inhibiting objective thinking, then
we will be able to go into the silence of this
mental developing room of subconsciousness
regardless of where we may happen to be —
while waiting at the station for a train, while
motoring, while afoot on the road, or in the
woods, or awake in bed, or even while attend-
ing to the routine of business, shop, or house-
hold affairs. In fact we see instances daily
of persons who practice this without consciously realizing it. We say such persons
are " absent-minded." This is true. They
are absent mentally in an *objective* sense even
while moving about in street, factory, business,
or amidst gay company. They are entirely
oblivious to all outward surroundings and activities because they place themselves in a subjective condition where they can dwell and be
with their cherished thought mentally. This
may or may not be an extreme suggested
method of keeping watch over our developing
picture, yet it shows that our whole thinking
is fixed upon our sunken thought; we show a
certain loyalty to it, and " loyalty is that
quality which prompts a person to be true to
the thing he undertakes."

The greatest dreams and greatest visions have been thus held before the mind while those who entertained them were engaged in arduous labor otherwise. There are moments given to all of us for reviewing our pictures in this manner, little intervals of time, and when we enter into the actual technique of our work we will not fail to make use of them.

CHAPTER XII

DEVELOPING PROCESS CAN BE FACILITATED

THIS reviewing time when we enter mentally into the great chemical laboratory and developing region of our subconsciousness to look at our mental picture, ought to be made a time of keen alertness and watchfulness; we ought to observe every friend who comes to us; examine every seemingly chance word; every invitation, every letter, every circumstance, every occasion, everything in fact which enters into and becomes a part of our daily work, play and life, since these are the separate and detached yet integral parts, unknown to us at the time, which will combine to bring about our picture as a whole.

In this way we are able consciously to co-operate in the developing process. We can facilitate it, and when we ourselves move consciously in the directions which become apparent to us, our understanding-thought will

116

become not only a center of attraction, drawing all things toward it, but a positive mentative force moving in the direction of our developing picture; a force which will express itself in enthusiasm, interest, attention, joy, effort and work. If these supreme moving elements are not present in visualizing, then our concepts remain mere dreams and, divine as they may be, they hardly can be expected to come into realization on the physical plane.

By saying that we must move in the direction of our developing picture, it is also meant that everything which we do, everything which we think or say, must at this time be made to suggest or relate itself to the outwardly *finished picture* of whatever we are visualizing. We must say, " I will read this book because it may show me the way to get the ten thousand dollars I need," or " This will make a dandy desk for my business," or " I am going to buy these curtains so I will have them for my home."

As we have already said, we must make the *mental reality* of our developing thought so clear to our consciousness, again and again, during the intervals of its review in our minds, that we will unconsciously and subjectively convey our thought to all other minds subjectively conditioned, and with whom we come in contact, since this is one of the avenues of its outworking.

We must remember that out of ourselves our thought has come, so that we are the very heart, the very center, the magnetized nucleus and the starting point of the projected thought which is in process of developing. Through us our imaged thought which is sent forth, assumes the nature of a fiat, enclothing itself in positive statements such as those we have just mentioned, and these statements appear from our own declarative lips as the first outward evidence of the existence of the yet scarcely outwardly observed picture in our minds. Following our declarative words, then our clothes, our inclinations, our studies, our pastimes, all will begin to accommodate themselves in the direction of our developing thought, so that we will begin to wear the tie and broad-brimmed hat of the artist before we ever obtain the money to attend an art school; we will frequent automobile salesrooms before even we have the requisite money to buy the auto; we will read up books on travel before the thought of traveling has worked itself out into a possibility, and we will spend our hours of pastime among machinery or among men who represent the thought of the business or the trade which is forming itself subconsciously within us. And in deliberate visualizing, as we move thus *consciously* in the direction of our developing understanding, we will find that other minds, carnate and incarnate, forces visible and invisible, or persons attuned to our thought by virtue of entertaining a corresponding thought of their own, will unconsciously or consciously move into the magnetic circle of our thought; they will fit themselves into and assist in its fulfillment as we are caused correspondingly to fit into and assist in the fulfillment of their own.

In true visualizing we are drawn into the lives of others as others are drawn into our lives; our thought is the magnetized center but in its attraction it draws or should draw those only to whom in turn it is attracted, and whose purpose in turn it may serve.

This should be part of our imaged thought at all times; it should be part of the light of true understanding of which our thought is composed, since in this is contained not only the mental ethics of visualizing, but the success of our work as well.

Finally let us not forget here, that while our imaged thought, launched forth into the ocean of the very universe of subjective consciousness, finds every *corresponding* friendly force, carnate and incarnate, visible and invisible, attracted to it, yet does it also meet at every turn, those forces visible and invisible which are its opposite in nature and which are ready on every occasion to exercise no inconsiderable activity and influence against the orderly and natural development of that which we seek to have become a part of our outward lives.

These forces may not always be *opposing* forces but sometimes *dominating, self-seeking* forces. It is well to observe that primitive minds of this type are stronger in any mental contest for the possession of any object in mind *based upon a material basis,* and almost inevitably overcome or come over the minds of a higher and more spiritual type. This is because the more elemental type of mind operates from the basis of pure desire or passion and consequently is a more vitalized and positive unit in the material direction in which it exerts itself. We see this so often displayed in the instance of the meek, the harmless and innocent who are irresistibly drawn at times into the scheme and picture of the designing, the worldly, the selfish and the carnal mind. The innocent dove among us is observed moving irresistibly in the direction of the fanged serpent; and the lamb into the very jaws of the devouring tiger. It seems to be the sacrificial mental tragedy of our upward and outward development, and will be so until the time when we can warn, protect and defend ourselves and others by the more powerful dissolving white light of the spirit against the conscious and unconscious mental processes of those who for the time attempt to neutralize, suspend, and dissolve our own outwardly forming picture and seek to cause us to step into and serve the purposes of their own.

Somewhat later we will learn just how to generate this white light so that it becomes possible so to sublimate our projected thought of what we want to be, or do, or have, so illumine and radiate it, that it becomes not only an " enlightened " thought but an " enlightening thought " containing within itself the white light of the higher form of understanding not only to guide our thought on its outward course, but to " enlighten " and make bright all that through which it moves, dispelling darkness and that which is a part of darkness.

When this is done, then we will find our developing picture shaping itself without interruption, and in an orderly and logical manner. Each time that we lift it, so to speak, from its chemical bath, we will find some further sign of development, some further trace of its outward appearance. We will find our understanding as a whole, shaping itself into an increasingly orderly and beautiful arrangement of events, incidents and occasions, following one another in uninterrupted logical sequence; and all of them transpiring for the purpose of bringing the good desire of our hearts nearer and nearer to the point of fulfillment in our outward lives.

Let us remember that in protecting ourselves against the subtile interference of other minds, we must in turn hold inviolate the principle never to include another mind *in formulating and developing our own thought-picture,* no matter how self-justified *we may feel, or how good our intentions, unless we have the full and willing consent of that other mind.*

This consideration not only is an ethical and moral one in our visualizing work, but a scientific one as well.

A photographer would not make bold to in-
corporate as a part of his photograph someone
who objected or refused to give his or her consent to be " taken " as a part of his picture.
Newspaper photographers devoid of any con-
siderations of this kind, and who have sur-
reptitiously sought by all kinds of questionable
methods to violate the rights of another in this
sense, have brought down the wrath of the of-
fended person, and sometimes a libel suit. In
visualizing it becomes a question not of incorporating another person, but *another mind,* or
part of another mind, unwilling or unsuspect-
ingly to become part of our own; literally
attempting in this manner to imprison, de-
prive, if not to rob the other mind of its individual freedom of action and expression.

This may be done quite innocently though
none the less unpermissibly by us. A mother,
let us say, with the best of intentions may attempt to formulate a picture relating to her
boy; a picture which assumes to regulate his
outward conduct according to her fixed ideas;
a lover may seek to visualize the other into his
or her life to a point where it becomes a mentally compulsory force depriving the other of
free action. A woman may seek to visualize a

certain person as a husband, or a man may seek
to visualize a certain person as his wife; but
the moment we do this without the consent of
the other mind, *we tamper with an independent intelligence* which normally is also formulating and outpicturing itself along its own
God-given lines of independent action and
understanding; probably in an entirely different or opposite direction; and since no two un-
like thought-images can associate or relate
themselves subjectively, an impasse results,
causing mental stress, inharmony, and unhap-
piness to both minds; or the involuntary sur-
render, temporarily, of the one understanding
to the other. In every instance it is criminal
and self-destructive of the mind which undertakes to misuse the visualizing power in this
sense, and in deliberate cases the power of
imaging and seeing is known to have been altogether lost, bringing about a mental blindness
in which no outpicturing at all becomes
possible.

PART III

TECHNIQUE OF VISUALIZING

CHAPTER I

PREPARING OUR THOUGHT-OBJECT
FOR REPRODUCTION

WE have now touched upon all the preliminaries involved in visualizing and with a thorough knowledge of these, we are possessed of the secret of our Aladdin's Lamp. We know the method of its operation, and we are ready to apply this method in bringing to us whatsoever in good we want to have, to be, or do.

We have confidently selected a certain *definite mental object* which by means of this method of *deliberate visualizing* has become the " *object of our heart's desire.*" It may be a much needed sum of money for ourselves or for someone whom we dearly love or want to help, it may be a home, it may be the establishment of a business, or it may be any other object in life which we want to bring into outward visibility.

Our formulating faculties have been at work specializing and differentiating our desire, it has been placed in the current of our objective thinking, and now has taken shape as an *object of thought* in the photographic studio of our objective minds.

Suppose we take three definite objects, all of which can be co-ordinated into what we may term the outpicturing of a career. Let these objects be five thousand dollars, a business and a home.

We now begin to condition ourselves mentally for this purpose. Our first consideration is the quiet, darkened room in some part of the house. This room will serve every mental purpose which we have covered in our preliminary studies — studio, dark chamber and developing room.

We remember that if such a room is not available, then our work can be carried on at night in bed just as effectively. In fact, the very early hours are best for our work, and wherever possible, the student should accommodate himself or herself to these hours.

Seating ourselves in a comfortable arm-chair which will permit the greatest possible relaxation, or reclining on a couch, or lying in bed, we begin our practical work by bringing the " object of our heart's desire "— our career — to mind.

We recall the fact that this action of the will requires as little strenuous effort as does the photographer in placing his object in a position where he can photograph it to the best advantage. In fact, if the object is *truly* desired, then it is " uppermost " in our minds and in that position soon makes its presence *felt* in our consciousness without any effort on our part.

CHAPTER II

POURING LIGHT UPON OUR THOUGHT–OBJECT

WE must remember that we " feel " our mental object before we see it. The entire process involved in establishing a thought-object in the mind and photographing it is almost so instantaneous that we are not consciously aware of any stages, and yet it is the incitement of the object in our mind which makes us " think about it " and upon it, as we sit in our darkened room, and this means that a steady stream of our thinking is being directed toward our objects in the same manner in which the sun's rays pour themselves about and upon material objects.

Moved by the gentle heat generated by our thinking, our mechanical faculties, the mechanical apparatus of the mind, which we have termed our mental camera, imperceptibly glides into action, and in this same instant, sitting in our darkened room, we behold the objects not outwardly but inwardly.

CHAPTER III

SEEING OUR THOUGHT-OBJECT IN REFLECTION

WE are seeing our objects now, not directly, but by means of the single inner mental eye of the mind's camera which has caught up, collected and transmitted the rays of our illumined thinking into the illumining chamber of our consciousness. We behold our objects there and study them by *means of reflection.*

Wherever we fix our look now in the darkness of the room — whether upon the wall or ceiling or floor, or when our physical eyes are closed, we will see the phenomenon of our objects *projecting* themselves. They will appear first as a disc of white light and then slowly and gradually resolve themselves into the objects contained in the mind. We are seeing our mental objects now as projected thoughts or *images of light,* capable for the moment of extension by reflection outside of ourselves.

Wonderful indeed is this phenomenon of the projective power of mind but it is only the beginning of a mental projection which will carry our thoughts later on to distances and places far beyond the range of our own limited vision.

CHAPTER IV

POURING MORE MENTAL–LIGHT UPON OUR THOUGHT

AS we sit in our " silence room " and contemplate our thought, we seek to make our reflection of it more clear by getting " more light " of understanding upon it, since the more understanding we can apply the more clear the subsequent impression will be.

Sitting quietly, we bring into play that informative or illuminative light which has become part of us as the result of observation and experience, or as the result of relating ourselves to the Universal Source of All-Understanding of which we are a part. From whatever source our " enlightenment " comes, we must pour all of it now at this time of reflection so that we may see our object in the clearest light possible.

The thought of money, business, home must be so illumined that in reflection we must see clearly all that which pertains to it. We must remember that we are dealing with *things,*

and that no matter how much we may sublimate them in our visualizing, they are yet
conditional, and for this reason *they are related to circumstances and conditions,* and
these circumstances and conditions *must be
known and seen and made to conform themselves* as a part of the picture of our career.

For instance, our five thousand dollars may
not really suffice for the enterprise we have in
mind; it may be of a nature which will not
permit much home life; it may require resi-
dence abroad, and those for whom we are
planning a home may not want to leave their
own present environment for various reasons
which must be taken into account. These are
circumstances and conditions which enter into
our picture and upon which the light of our
understanding must be poured.

Then too, we must be familiar, by means of
outward observation and experience, with the
things which relate themselves to our inner
picture. If our thought of five thousand dollars is a vague one, then before we try to see it
clearly in mind, we must go to the bank and
ask the teller to show us five one-thousand
bills, or fifty one-hundred bills, which we study
carefully, and in this way, we get " more

light " upon the money; we are able to *see* it mentally more clearly.

So with the business enterprise. If it is an automobile business we have in mind, we visit automobile factories and observe the method of building an automobile.

So with the home. We visit the homes of our friends, we become acquainted with the various kinds of architecture, the kinds of brick and timber, the arrangement of rooms and every other detail which will help to " throw light " upon the thought of the home which we are contemplating now.

However, there is a yet finer, rarer light of understanding which we will now apply; an " enlightenment " which will make our reflected thought of money, business and home ever so much more clear for impressive purposes, and which will bring us ever so much more positive results.

We stimulate this finer light of understanding when in our contemplation we ask ourselves, " Why do I want the five thousand dollars, the business, the home? ", and when we answer this question from the inner spiritual source of all-light of our being, we bring a flood of illumination upon our projected thought.

We now begin to see our thought about the money, the business, the home in an " entirely different light," as we say. We see now that it is not the *thing* which we want but rather that which the *thing* symbolizes. It is not the outer object but the *inner* object which we are in the process of bringing forth.

What is this *inner object* or *purpose?* It is not the money but the *power* which money symbolizes; it is not the business but the means it provides us for extending our *good* will to others, and for providing *happiness* to those whom we love; it is not the home, the building of brick or timber, but the *comfort,* the *peace,* the *love,* the *joy,* the domestic *felicity,* the *shelter* and *protection* which a home represents or should represent.

✓   The more we see our objects in this light of spiritual understanding, the more inspired we become, and this inspired thinking provides the radiant and luminous mental light whereby our object becomes crystal clear to us.

CHAPTER V

ESTABLISHING OUR CORRECT VIEWPOINT

WHAT is more, this finer light of our higher understanding enables us now to establish our true viewpoint toward our thought.

Unless of an unusually spiritually endowed or instructed mind, we would have viewed our purpose in securing five thousand dollars, or a business, or a home, as the average mind views these things. We would have viewed them simply as *things*. We might have looked upon the five thousand dollars merely as a means to establishing a business for the purpose of *making more money* so that we could have plenty to spend not only for the purchase of a home, but for many other *things,* and these *things* we may merely have desired as a means of gratifying our pride, our vanity, our selfishness, our lust or any inverted or secondary relative cause in mind.

But now we view our imaged thought from an entirely different viewpoint, so that we know that what we want is really not the *thing,* which after all is a very elementary and limited object, involving circumstances and conditions, but *we want that which the thing symbolizes or represents*; we want, in so far as the money is concerned, the *power* to be and to have and to do the good we have in mind. We realize that money is simply the circulating medium, the symbol of value by means of which we are empowered to negotiate for that which is necessary in establishing our business and our home, and for accomplishing those purposes which are best carried out in our business and home.

Besides giving us the means of performing service, it will give us the occasion to employ and help others; it will make us the means of distribution of something which others need.

In the manner that our money represents *power,* so, as we have already seen, our business represents *service,* and other mental values; and in like manner our *home symbolizes comfort, shelter, love, protection,* and those other qualities which we usually associate with the thought of home.

We think of our home as a place where we are going to invite our friends as guests, where they are going to find mental and spiritual as well as material comforts, where we are going to exercise all those virtues which will serve for our own life-expansion and that of others.

In a word, we now see these so-called *things* reflected in our minds not simply as *things,* but as the very underlying understanding of our being, formed and projected and ready to be brought forth into our outward lives; our understanding-light has shaped itself into the forms of money, business and home, and this understanding-light is made up of the prismatic *qualities* or *causes* which in this way become embodiments of power, service, goodwill, protection, love, comfort, harmony, peace and joy in us and through us.

Taking this viewpoint we need have no more concern with the impressiveness of our object and its power to reproduce itself.

CHAPTER VI

FOCUSING UPON OUR IMAGED THOUGHT

WITH proper light and a right viewpoint toward our thought, we focus our *whole* attention upon it, bearing in mind that we are now focusing not on the five thousand dollars, the business and the home, but upon the *qualities of joy, love, protection, peace and happiness* of which these mental objects are merely symbols.

These qualities have taken shape simply so that we can see and get their reflection for purposes of outward reproduction.

Let us also bear in mind that this concentration does not imply a tension or strained effort of the will, but rather an easy and pleasant exercise.

We have said that concentration upon *one single object of thought* does not mean necessarily that our thought must be comprised of only one *thing*; it may take in a number of things so long as they are directly related and serve to make a *complete* picture, and this is so in the instance of the career which we are outpicturing. The five thousand dollars as we have already said is for the purpose of financing our business enterprise, and our business enterprise is for the purpose, among other good purposes, of providing a suitable home for those whom we love. We see how every one of these objects is a very essential and related part of our thought, and we should not hesitate to allow whatever other thoughts of a related kind that come to us, to image themselves, and to become, as they will, part of the good picture of our career.

Thus in our thought of the business, we may plan perhaps to include a brother; or a sister; we may make it a corporation in which we can include several of our friends; we may include an automobile which will serve both our business and our pleasure.

What we aim to avoid now is the intrusion of any vagrant thoughts which may and will seek to enter within the magic circle where our one definite thought is held. We must allow no fear thought, no opposing thought, no worry-thoughts, no alien thought of any kind to enter through our mental-camera eye, but rather must we keep our eye *single* to the one true thought of our career.

CHAPTER VII

IMPRESSING OUR IMAGED THOUGHT

HAVING the best possible *quality* and *quantity* of higher understanding reflecting the five thousand dollars, the business and the home; having a scientifically correct focus and viewpoint, our career now will be imaged forth in a form of understanding-light which will permit the *very finest* impression to be made upon our subjective thinking-substance.

We have seen that our money, our business, and our home *is good* for us to have, and in the moment in which we truly acknowledge and recognize this fact mentally, our thought will become an *impressive* one. It will make its impression upon us in the finest and most definite way possible. The shutter of the mind is voluntarily and momentarily lifted, the full light of our understanding moves into and impresses itself upon the sensitized film of our subjective thinking; it takes on the qualities of this subjective thinking and becomes en-

filmed and sealed in the subjective; undergo-
ing a silent, invisible inner development, or
reduction on its way toward ultimate matter,
and however infinitely inconceivable this reduction is, we can say that it is now becoming
a more dense form than the pure form of
mental light was before impression. We are
now ready to follow our imaged thought in the
next stage of its outward development.

CHAPTER VIII

OUR THOUGHT IMPRESSION IN SOLUTION

WE now consider our imaged thought as
having passed into the developing room
of subconsciousness; to that place in mind,
or state of mind which precludes all outer vibrations of objective thinking.

Let us remember that at this time of transference of our thought-image, we are resting
quietly and in an entirely relaxed attitude,
mentally and physically. We have entered
into a subjective mental condition, becoming

as nearly passive as possible and refraining
from any further thinking upon our " impressed " thought-image.   There is no need
for it.   The light of our understanding has
passed from the objective phase of mind and
is slowly and gently submerging itself in the
chemical developing solution of our subsense-
consciousness.

The student remembers at this moment what
our impressed thought really is; it is a specialized form of mental light; *the light of our understanding,* which has become enfilmed or
" impressed " and has now become sunk in
the very deep of our individualized subsense-
consciousness where it becomes a " center of
attraction " for the infinitely inconceivable
polarized mentoids which are contained in
this chemical solution of mind.

Resting in our passive or subjective attitude,
a great calm comes over us at this moment; a
great feeling of assurance and peace, and in
most instances we fall into a restful, natural
sleep.   That is as it should be.   In the few
moments in which the transference has occurred, the outer faculties have performed
their function.   The inner subjective and subconscious phase of mind is now at work and

further formulation of our mental picture of the money, the business and the home, has begun.

A law of development is at work. It is not our individualized objective consciousness which is now busy with our career, but our subjective consciousness working upon and worked upon by our understanding which is now gathering together for itself and around its delicate form of light the further mental chemical structure for its outward manifestation.

Our objective attitude of mind from this point on becomes, as we know, simply one of *co-operation,* and this co-operation is exemplified best when our thinking and acting in all our daily outward affairs is directed continually in ways which will facilitate the development of our thought.

We must have an understanding faith in the outcome of our developing picture; we must henceforth be true and loyal to the subjective forces working for us; we must be mentally alert to their direction; we must be patient; we must help by " getting into the spirit " of our picture; we must *love* it, as it were, into existence.

But separate from this we know that a movement of the underlying natural forces of this substance of our subconscious thinking or mind-solution now has been started in motion, carrying our projected understanding or thought with them, not only to the very depths of our own individualized subconsciousness but to all other minds which are for the moment subjectively conditioned to our thinking, until our thought is carried out and submerged into the very ocean of universal subsense-consciousness, attracting unto itself not only other thoughts but taking hold on the subsense side of all those things, circumstances, conditions and persons that are to be a part of its outward fulfillment.

CHAPTER IX

REVIEWING OUR DEVELOPING PICTURE FROM TIME TO TIME

THE whole mental-mechanical and, to an extent, the mental-chemical process connected with the visualizing of our career, has

perhaps taken from ten to thirty minutes of
quiet contemplation and reflection in our
" silence room," depending upon the time
which we have taken to get comfortably settled,
and to concentrate upon our object.

Now, however, since our thought-image is
submerged, not only in our individualized subconsciousness but in the universal subconsciousness of which our own is an inseparable
part, it becomes a matter of development which
may take hours, days, and even years to fulfill itself, depending upon certain mental laws
which we apply, as well as upon the various
modifications of those agencies which will in-
troduce themselves, and which include ourselves, other minds, and those circumstances
and conditions to which we must react, *even
though we subjectively control them.* For this
reason we have ample time from day to day
to go into our darkened room which we now
term our " developing room," settling ourselves as comfortably as possible, letting ourselves relapse into the subjective state
completely, and spending as much time there
as we find our moods and daily affairs will
allow.

In these moments, we mentally lift our en-

filmed-thought of our career from its subjective bath, and quietly meditate upon it and
review its progress subjectively, always remembering, however, that our examination of
our mental picture is possible at any time and
anywhere — at a railroad station, in a train,
or while at work, and if we are true to our
picture, we will find ourselves doing this, as we
said before, without being consciously aware
of the fact.

CHAPTER X

WATCHING FOR OUTWARD INDICATIONS

DAY by day, or night by night, in our
quiet room or wherever and whenever
we enter mentally into this subjective contemplation of our developing thought, we find
ourselves patiently and lovingly and yet
vigilantly watching for the first early outward
indications and traces of our developing
picture, knowing that here as elsewhere, we
must " learn to labor and to wait." If we are
anxious, it is now *not the anxiety implied by*

fear or worry or doubt about the outcome, but rather an attitude which is best described as an attitude of eager expectancy hard to restrain; if we are intense, it is not the nervous tension or tenseness of impatience, but rather an eagerness to know how our reproduction fares, and we know, or should know, that it fares well.

Alone, in our subdued and darkened room, which is the best place for reviewing the progress of our picture, we sit and examine the *outward appearing evidences* of it, remembering that our developing understanding really is launched forth now beyond the circumscribed and limited scope of individualized subconsciousness; beyond the limits of ourselves as units of mind-light, and that it is *developing as an enfilmed form of mental light in that great universal everywhere of subjective subconsciousness of which we are an inseparable part,* formulating a structure of infinitely delicate texture out of this body-forming substance every moment and every hour now.

Realizing as we do that our submerged understanding is now precipitated in this ocean of chemicalized mind-substance which underlies and pervades *all conditions* and *all circum-stances* of this outward world, we watch for indications *everywhere and in everything;* looking upon friends, relatives, strangers, books, words, occasions and all else which seemingly happens to come within the develop-ing area of our outwardly forming picture but which in reality is attracted to it by the de-veloping law which is at work.

Unexpected persons, perhaps, from a dis-tance, having affinity or subjective kinship to our thought of money, business and home, now come to us in a seemingly miraculous manner. Seemingly trifling bits of information drift into our daily affairs, casual words are said, books are loaned to us, letters are received, and a hundred and one incidents of a like kind transpire, which manifest solely for the pur-pose of becoming a part of our forming picture.

As we quietly and meditatively review our picture with this fact in mind, we find perhaps a first faint indication of its outward develop-ment in the appearance of a distant friend who comes into our lives and whom we have not seen in many years; or of a stranger we have never before seen; or in the form of an unexpected letter; or in the form of a casual introduction at the club or elsewhere.

The distant friend may have returned as a man or woman of means, and in the course of a conversation may casually mention the fact that he or she has some five thousand dollars in cash for investment. Probably we are asked if we know of a good local proposition, and instantly the remark relates itself to our own need for five thousand dollars; the stranger may be looking to enter into a business in our part of the city or town which is similar to that with which our own thought is concerned; the unexpected letter may contain a check which will serve as an initial payment on the merchandise necessary for our business, and our casual introduction may lead to a further introduction to a cashier or director of a bank who can provide the needed finances.

Even while the picture of our money and business is forming itself in this wise, the associated object of a home for which our business will provide the means is also forming itself in perhaps a very remote though none the less tangible way. Someone may give us some tapestries, someone a beautiful set of dishes; a catalogue of homes may come to us as the most remote indication; and so, as we watch our outworking thought from day to day, taking account of it as it were, we find our career is beginning to work out most wonderfully, yet simply, " just as we had pictured it."

There is nothing remarkable, mystical, supernatural or even unusual about this " working out " of our picture. It simply is a chain of sequences or consequences which are continually entering into and passing out of our lives unnoticed except that in deliberate visualizing we become keenly conscious and alert as to their appearance and presence, and in this recognition we " make the most " out of them, as we should.

CHAPTER XI

STRENGTHENING OUR DEVELOPING THOUGHT

WE must remember that our mental-chemical developing formula calls for the introduction of all the developing agents which will serve to " bring out " our picture in all its clearest and finest details and in the quickest possible time; so that we bring to the developing process all the interest, all the joy, all the gladness that a keen anticipation implies. In a word, it calls for *feeling,* and every bit of feeling that we possibly can generate and discharge now into the developing solution of sub-consciousness, strengthens it!

We must " enter into the spirit " of our picture, for this is what our picture actually is — *SPIRIT* — and by *spirit* we mean that true substance of which we have spoken throughout our lessons and from which all things whatsoever hidden or revealed, are formed.

We must get into the *livingness* of our

career, *we must feel* its magnetic warmth, its
life; remembering the fact that with this
mental-chemical modification, we are bringing
into outward manifestation now, not that
which has no life, but *that which is LIFE.*

We " get into the feeling " of our picture
and facilitate activity of development innerly,
not merely by using our imagination, but by
our actual outward sense of touch. While
seated quietly in our " developing room " we
take several bills of any denomination and
pass them from one hand to another, just as
the bank teller does in counting bills which he
ʳeceives or hands out through the little window.
We " feel " the texture of the bills, we " feel "
their smoothness or roughness as the case may
be, and in this way the *inward reality* of our
feeling finds itself more quickly corresponding to the *outward reality* into which our
thought of money is shaping itself.

So with the business which we are developing mentally. If it is an automobile business,
then we want to know how it " feels " to handle
a prospective customer, and so we talk to our
friends and try to sell them a machine; we
wax enthusiastic about the car to such a point
where our friends will almost be ready to buy

the automobile on the strength of what we say. We can, if we choose, offer our services to some sales concern without charge, if necessary, and in this way we not only "feel" our way into the business, but we get "into the spirit" of the "selling game" as it is called. In doing this we *must feel* the happiness, the joy, and the interest of selling; we must *feel* that selling automobiles, or whatever other outward form our business is to take, is the one thing which we have wanted to do all our lives, and this means that we *love* it.

Let us remember always that our career is formulating, specializing, and providing expression for itself not only through the brain of us *but through the heart of us also;* so that we are introducing into our formula now, not only the elements of *interest, joy and gladness,* but the element of *love* — the element which, charged into subconsciousness, contains not only the warmth but the mothering and nurturing qualities as well.

Happy, indeed, are we if we are able to make this mental-chemical charge of *love* into our subconscious developing solution a great and overwhelming one; a *love* for our career that will dissolve any element not related to

it, and " fix " our career in a manner which
will make it permanent and true. Knowing
the worthy purpose for which our money is
desired, we are able to transmute and chemi-
calize our thought of it until our love enters
into its very metal when it makes its outward
appearance in our career. So with our business. Knowing the worthy purpose which it
is to serve in providing the means of happiness for others, we come to *love* it even before
it has materialized outwardly; and in a similar manner we *feel* the *greatest love* toward
the thought of our home. We go to a furniture
establishment and there thrill inwardly as we
lovingly handle piece after piece of furniture,
or this or that rug which we "*feel*" *and*
know will be ours in a little while to come,
even as it is already ours in spirit; or we walk
about in other homes and say to ourselves,
" This is how *my* home shall be "; saying it
not only lovingly but with all the feeling, con-
viction and assurance which our understanding faith has given unto us.

The more of this element of love for our
career which we can continually pour into the
solution of our subconsciousness, the more
responsive, giving, and yielding its forming

substance will be to our attracting thought
which is taking shape in it, and the more fixed
and permanent will the outcome be, for *this
is the power and nature of love.*

Let us feel toward our whole developing
career the same great and overwhelming love,
the same joy of anticipation, which thrills
and floods the being of the expectant mother;
remembering rejoicingly that the enfilmed
light of our best understanding, our best wisdom is sunk in the only real substance that is
or ever will be, and that it is there incarnating
itself into that which from now on will make
itself more and more evident outwardly in
our lives, until the day when our money, our
business and our home or whatever else in this
life we choose to see, becomes an outwardly
accomplished fact.

CHAPTER XII

CONCLUSION

WE would feel remiss indeed if we concluded these lessons without offering to the student a higher concept of the purpose of visualizing than that which generally is accepted as justification for the use of the visualizing power.

We hold this power to be holy and divine, a form of the one and only Power which is, and in this thought we feel that its use should be *consecrated,* serving first in the divine unfoldment of ourselves in good, and then, through us, serving in the unfoldment of the good in all.

The very best and the very highest that we can ever hope to obtain by the use of visualizing can never carry us beyond this two-fold object. In fact, the whole photographic apparatus of the mind, its imaging and formulative devices, as well as the mental-chemical process of development, can only serve, and *must,* even though unconsciously, serve this high purpose in the end.

How much better then, to carry out this object in a *conscious* way, knowing that we are using this power for the very divine purpose of visualizing ourselves into all that we want to be, or do, or have *in good,* and knowing further that in picturing ourselves thus *in good* we are outpicturing ourselves *in God.* In the very highest sense, we are not only outpicturing ourselves *in God,* but God is outpicturing Himself in us and through us. The more unselfish we make our object in visualizing, the more will this divine unfoldment manifest itself to us in the outward good or God of all.

It is with this highest concept in mind that we leave the student to apply his or her knowledge of visualizing to good ends, confident that the outcome of the picture conceived in good cannot be anything else but successful in its outward reproduction.

In the same manner in which this book has served YOUR *purpose, so let it serve the purpose of others whom you would like to help by having them read it.*

PASS IT ON!

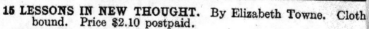